Revenge!

Revenge!

Don't Get Mad, Get Even

George Hayduke

Lyle Stuart Inc.   Secaucus, N.J.

Copyright© 1982 by Paladin Press
All rights reserved
Published by Lyle Stuart Inc.
120 Enterprise Ave., Secaucus, N.J. 07094
In Canada: Musson Book Company,
A division of General Publishing Co. Limited
Don Mills, Ontario
Manufactured in the United States of America
ISBN 0-8184-0353- 5

Originally published under the title Up Yours!

"Everyone wants revenge," Jack Burns says, "That's natural."
　　　　　　　　　　　　　　　　—Edward Abbey,
　　　　　　　　　　　　　　　　Good News

Contents

Revenge!

Let's Share a Few Thoughts

One of history's funnier artists was the late Hugh Troy. He once said that his favorite fantasy stunt entailed buying out the entire orchestra section of the Metropolitan Opera House on opening night of some high-brow affair. By Troy's fiendish prearrangement, every person at the show would have a head of thick, black hair. That is, everyone except for a group of bald men, who would be seated in a very special arrangement. When viewed from the balcony, their bald heads would spell out one of his favorite four-letter words.

"I wasn't angry with anyone special; I just wanted to shock hell out of all the pickle-personality snobs. Besides, think of *my* fun, and how many people would be amused and not insulted," Troy said later.

Hugh Troy dreamed up his fantasy in a simpler time when people were much more civilized in their behavior toward each other I would probably have been happier back then, too. But unlike Ronald Reagan and others of his ilk, I cannot afford to put my head in some rich friend's corporate sandbox and pretend it's 1949 again. Let's talk today.

Just about every single day, everyone except for the most obtuse functional illiterate encounters situations where someone or some institution or business tries to take unfair advantage of us. Or, having trusted someone with our money, time, or love, we suffer the consequences of uncaring incompetence.

Think about it. You can probably recall hundreds of times when you were insulted, stepped on, or ripped off. You didn't speak up to protect your interests, possessions, property, reputation, or those of people you like and love. You were afraid, or maybe just timid.

It is sad to think that this sort of royal screwing is such a common experience for Americans today. And here we have the reason why I wrote my first book on this topic: *Getting Even: The Complete Book of Dirty Tricks.* My beautifully incorrigible readers were then treated to a follow-up volume of vengeful trickery: *Getting Even 2: More Dirty Tricks from the Master of Revenge.* I don't know who dreamed up that "Master of Revenge" moniker. I think it's just that I was the first person who was gutsy and crazy enough to seriously address this issue—which threatens every man and woman among us.

Anyway, *Revenge!* is meant to fill the gap in sophistication evident in the previous *Getting Even* books. Just as plastic vomit is now old hat, so are some of the gags and scams I cooked up in the other two books. So my readers and I have put our evil little pea brains together to come up with this collection of advanced harassment and revenge techniques. They are specifically meant to meet the challenge of getting even in the eighties. Here you have it.

If you still believe that the meek shall inherit the earth, wake up and grow up. It's too late for that dream. But, there's still time for you to protect your own personal space and environment. You don't do that by being an indecisive wimp, either. The bullies instantly eat wimps, do-gooders, and other cheek-turners for a one bite mini-snack.

Is getting back at people useful? Will it clear up your complexion? Your ulcers? Robert G. Wheaton writes, "From time to time I strike back and get the satisfaction of vengeance. But, there are many times that it is sufficiently gratifying just to know that if I really wanted to deal some SOB some misery, I'm now well armed with the required knowledge. That way I can just blow off or ignore the minor nuisances and concentrate on the truly 'needy' among enemies."

There are a lot of unhappy folks who refuse to be stomped on. The wimpy Earl Keese of *Neighbors* fame is being replaced by folks like the Rev. J. Richard Young of Sun Valley, Arizona who writes, "Around here no one rips me off, but I am known to be fair and honest. I have been a dedicated *Getting Even* person since a garage ripped me off twelve years ago. I put them out of business in two months. I never use violence or resort to things which cause physical injury. I prefer mental torture as it leaves no scars that show and is nearly impossible to prosecute."

The growing army of revenge-seekers ranges from unrepentant practical jokers to out-and-out grim reapers. David Havoc of Omaha says, "I'm very happy to discover kindred spirits and that some of your plots are not only hatched and pulled off by others than myself, but that in many circles, it is considered a point of honor to get back at these bullies who make our lives miserable."

As the bizarro rock band Devo said, "You'll never live it down unless you whip it up."

Getting even has four big advantages, according to Jimi the Z of Kansas City, one of my most prolific contributors. His four are:

1. It gives you the personal satisfaction of not having been beaten.
2. It is a big deterrent to anyone repeating their offense against you or anyone else.
3. It is fun for you and educational for both sides—you *and* the mark.
4. It might make some rotten people decent if they knew they couldn't get away with being bullies.

There were some readers who wanted more sophistication, adjudication, and humane selectivity. For instance, some folks wrote to plead a degree of ethics and humanity. One man, who wants to be known simply as Jack S. from San Francisco, wrote that I should "maintain a certain degree of ethics, i.e., treat your mark with as much humanity as he or she deserves."

I think I made that point in my first book, and I still agree. It's important to make your revenge fit the crime. But, as Jack points out, "Do not get caught up in worrying too much about your mark. In other words, don't let your own conscience screw you. . . . Punishments should fit the crime."

Charles Platt questions my inclusion of both harmless and lethal stunts without differentiation. I assume he means some sort of product safety warning, ranking revenge scams in terms of potential effect. Mr. Platt writes, "I enjoyed your book, though I question your decision to include harmless pranks and lethal revenge tactics side by side, as if there isn't any difference. Even in the field of illegal revenge, there should be some scheme of values."

He is correct. On the other hand, I feel uncomfortable making value judgments for others. Each of us must decide for ourselves not only what is right or wrong, but also what is "just right" and what constitutes "too much." The majority of my readers are out for a belly laugh, or they are folks who feel a sense of relief and reward just reading how someone else got even. Yet many readers *do* use these stunts, putting my suggestions to "good purpose," whatever that means. Personally, I believe in the Golden Rule; I really do. I also don't think this belief is at all inconsistent with anything in this book.

At the risk of seeming a nag, which my friends tell me I am, please let me beg you not to get even without provocation. There is enough nastiness, ill will, and violence—both physical and mental—in our world without adding senseless revenge to it. And, don't be a bully. Some of the stunts in this book are dangerous and should not be used by those with a single-digit IQ. As Bob Dylan said some years ago before his mind died and went straight, "Those who live outside the law must really be honest."

GEORGE HAYDUKE

How to Use This Book

by M. Wellsley Spofford, Ph.D.

Mr. Hayduke asked me to write a foreword to his book, but I felt that too much pedagogical rhetoric would only cloud its definitive purpose, which is far beyond replication of his earlier philosophies. Instead, I opted to produce this methodological supplement for the reader's pragmatic edification.

As before, Mr. Hayduke has arranged his chapters both by subject and method, then arranged these alphabetically. In addition to searching chapter headings, he suggests you search other specific areas as many of the items lend themselves to more than one treatment. Indeed, in his classic review of Mr. Hayduke's original two books, Dr. Millard Plankton, the renowned professor of Arcaneology at Louisiana School of Divinity, notes that some serious scholars of "Hayduking" have compiled extensive cross-indices of the various combinations of our author's classifications of marks/stunts/materials/methods, et cetera. Mr. Hayduke himself suggests that each reader perform an informal search or working cross-index of his or her own while using this book.

In the author's own words, "If you have a problem with some person or institution or whatever, look to the chapter heading of this book for an appropriate response in solving your problem through the use of creative revenge. Look at some other headings, too, and you'll get more ideas to escalate your deserved revenge."

I can easily concur with that. Here, then, is Mr. Hayduke's newest book. Please, gentle reader, enjoy yourself.

Additives

Heidi and Hamilton, the dynamic duo from Canoga Park, have cooked up a delightful additive for your mark's soup. It's called jimsonweed, a flowering vine growing in Southern California and many other regions around the U.S. While the leaves are quite poisonous, the root is certainly bizarre, or at least it causes that sort of behavior. According to Heidi, it is from the *Datura* family and was used by local Indians for getting buzzed.

In any case, Hamilton chopped some root into very fine pieces and put it into their soup, without Heidi's knowledge. She picks up the sad tale.

"Half an hour after eating I was tired and dizzy. In an hour I had the worst case of cotton mouth ever . . . gallons of water didn't even touch it. Soon after, I had the whirlies, like I was really drunk. This high wasn't pleasant at all, because by now both of us were sicker than dogs with nonstop dry heaves. It lasted into the next morning, and I had blurred vision the whole day. Hamilton said he used about one-third cup of chopped jimsonweed to three quarts of lentil soup. Wow!"

The Dean of the Hayduke College of Pharmacology, Sambo Anderson, says jimsonweed is poisonous and can be acutely hallucinogenic. He cautions that if you must use it, boil out the poison, use sparingly, and then, only on a truly rotten mark.

As in my past books, a reader passes along yet another additive for Preparation H. Bill from New Orleans suggests adding superglue. I have no idea if this is even feasible. He swears that it will work. I'm afraid to ask. Superglue? Hey, man, that's piling insult on injury.

If for some reason you want to keep your mark on the move, you can add mineral oil to his/her coffee. Roger Orlando suggests you do this in steadily increasing amounts until the correct posture for the mark is achieved.

Air Polluters

This one's strictly for the minor league, neighborhood polluter, the small-timer whose smoky house chimney looks like the whole Indian nation is sending a smoke signal from his fireplace. Or try it on a small industrial plant where the roof and chimney stack have fairly easy access. Davey Jones dips into his nasty locker for an actual story.

"We had this neighbor who used to burn garbage in his fireplace. I think his specialty was burning old dead animals. The gunk that poured out of that man's chimney would give soot a good name. It made Gary, Indiana, look like God's country.

"The fallout, both particulate and odorous, was terrible all over the neighborhood. There were complaints to the authorities, petitions, neighborly persuasion visits. Nothing worked.

"Then, one night when he was out, we got up on his roof and poured soft tar down his chimney stack. He was gone two days, came back, and fired up his fireplace. After about ten minutes, the fiery heat ignited the soft tar coating we'd given his chimney . . . WHOOMM and WOOOSHHH, it looked like a combination of a Roman candle and a direct hit on a fuel dump in a war movie.

"The fire company got there in time to prevent serious damage, and the fire marshal gave him hell because of the situation. Everyone blamed the man for burning crap in there all those months. He moved out of the neighborhood shortly after that."

Arson

Nobody seriously planning a torch job needs any of my help. It's America's fastest growing cottage industry. However, maybe you just want to create the illusion of an unsuccessful, but serious, attempt at arson. If you can then bring it to the attention of the insurance underwriter, it can be all the better for you and your mark.

Perhaps you are an ex-employee, terminated unfairly to make an opening for an "affirmative action" type of replacement, or you were framed by some other employees in a cover-up. If you feel you have a serious grievance, maybe you'd like to let your mark, the police, or his insurance company think that his place almost went "poof." With arson now a major crime wave, you can be sure the mark's insurance will get terminated.

Normally, a professional torch will set a lot of little blazes. Even though that's the way a pro works, it wouldn't be a good idea to use that M.O. because you want to create the illusion that the only reason the arson failed was because the time-delay incendiary never ignited and a call from a passerby (that's you) to the fire department thwarted the arsonist.

An often used time-delay incendiary is simply a book of matches with a burning cigarette jammed between the cover and back row of matchheads. In ten minutes, the cigarette burns down, the matches ignite, the gasoline-soaked rags underneath bloom into flame, and the arsonist is long gone. Next goes the structure. That's real arson.

However, if you light a cigarette and immediately stick it inside a small container, such as a cigar tube, the cigarette will be starved for oxygen and go out. Now you're ready to prepare your unsuccessful, evidential, incendiary device. Wedge the cigarette in the matchbook with the burned-out end sticking out. Collect an appropriate amount of cigarette ashes to drop under the cigarette at the "arson" scene. Leave this device at the scene, sitting on top a pile of gasoline-soaked rags that can't be traced back to you. Depart.

Now, call the fire department. Use Haydukery to disguise your voice because the call will certainly be recorded. Metropolitan police and fire departments routinely record all incoming calls. During an investigation of attempted arson, it is quite likely the victim will get to listen to the tape to see if he recognizes the caller's voice. Enough said.

Automobiles

Many camheads and antivehicular guerrillas must read my books, or else they are more prolific than the rest of you. Without fail, the heaviest amounts of mail come from readers who want to share nasty things you can do to automobiles. Many stunts were duplicated, and a few were totally without humor or redeeming revenge value, so they are not included here.

Maybe I should have named this book *Auto Madness*. It seems everyone has something nasty to do to every mark's car. E.W. from Hastings (a funny name), Nebraska, is a perfect example of motoring meanness. He writes, "George, try dropping a handful of BBs or lead shot down the carburetor of your mark's car . . . big, big, big repair bills."

Next, E.W. wants you to drain the oil from the mark's automobile. Replace the plug, then fill the crankcase with water. He says this will do more damage than simply letting the oil run out. E.W. says this works well because the oil warning lamp will not come on, yet the engine doesn't have any oil—which it needs so badly. Wasn't it in the Bible where I read that oil and water don't mix?

I'm sure all you motorheads and straights enjoyed the scene in *American Graffiti* where Officer Holstein has the rear end ripped out from under his cruiser. The movie is history, but modern technology now makes it easier than ever to recreate that scene for real. It works for any mark, not just those of the law enforcement persuasion.

Our Kansas City whiz, Jimi the Z, cautions that you do this to nobody but a truly mortal foe because it is so devastatingly expensive.

"You need some quarter-inch Kevlar rope, which is fairly lightweight, almost invisible at night, but stronger than hell. Attach one end around both axle sides with a double half-hitch. Leave twenty-five feet or so of slack, then attach the other end to a cement post, steel lightpole, or something that isn't going anywhere when the vehicle tries to.

"Believe me, this is fantastic to watch, to see the results. It almost always totals the car, as the entire rear end suspension is destroyed with great frame damage as well," Jimi writes with glee.

Meanwhile, there is more to fuel the imagination. Herb Bobwander is a real sweetie when it comes to sugaring your mark's gas tank. He says, "Sugar itself is messy and hard to pour into a tank. That's why I always use sugar cubes. Just a few in the old gas tank, and his MPG will drop to zilch, his car will stall out all the time and behave like a lemon-colored dog." Gee, Herb, you sound just like a commercial . . . for Hayduking a car.

If your mark has given you gas pains or a bellyache and you have access to his car, let's next add Sam Stein's fuel to the fires of your revenge. Sam says to take your hacksaw and cut off about three inches of the pipe leading to the car's gas tank.

"Do it a few inches from the top of the tank so all the gas doesn't spill out. Also, leave at least six inches of pipe connected to the gas tank well opening at the car body.

"Take a length of black plastic tubing about three feet long, attach it to the upper pipe, and secure it with a clamp. Run the rest of it down under the car so the end points to the right of the car. Secure this under the car with wires and string. Then, cut the tubing about six inches from the side of the car, so nobody will spot it."

Sam says that when the mark goes into the gas station to fill 'er up, he's in for a surprise. As most gas jockeys just lock the nozzle

and walk away, thinking it will automatically stop . . .
well . . . there should be about fifty dollars of gasoline on the
ground before anyone realizes something is wrong.

On the other hand, if he just puts in a few dollars worth, the
mark may not notice the puddle from his misdirected gas supply
line and will soon run out of gas. Let's hope it's miles from the
nearest station.

Either the American Mothball Marketing Association or fifty
readers had the same idea. It seems that ten or fifteen mothballs
popped into an auto's gas tank does an amazing job of murdering
its engine. Unlike sugar, these little timebombs dissolve
completely in gasoline, so there is no visible evidence. This one
sounds like big bills at the repair shop.

If you place a judicious amount of plaster of Paris in someone's
automobile carburetor it will at least keep the butterfly valve
open and that's at the very least, says Elmo Lang of Zanesville, Ohio.

This idea is untried but seems chemically sure, according to
Alexander Hogg of Tampa. He says that an ordinary Tampax
stuffed into a diesel fuel tank will dissolve into extremely fine
fibers which will clog filters and injection pumps. It seems as if
that would be a bloody nuisance to the engine's owner.

Putting additives in the crankcase is old hat. Instead, put things
in with the transmission fluid. If the mark's car is an automatic,
many of the fuel and oil additives mentioned in the earlier books
will also destroy the transmission. Or, as Todd Proudfoot
advocates, you can dissolve a bit of paraffin wax in ethlene glycol.
It will stop any auto transmission.

Wilson R. Drew provided two very positive and negative
numbers to be used for your mark's automobile. His first idea is
to switch the No. 1 and No. 8 wires in the firing order on the
distributor cap of a vehicle with an automatic transmission. You
will find these wires marked by number. This will allow the
vehicle to start either in "Neutral" or "Park" positions, but will
kill the engine as soon as the shift lever is put into "Drive." It will

happen repeatedly and cause all sorts of expensively fun problems for the mark, and profit for some mechanic.

Mr. Drew's second idea involves people who want to touch your car, such as hoodlums, thieves, and other street scum that you want to keep away. Get a coil from a Ford Model A car and have it hooked up by a competent and friendly mechanic. He hooks it to your car in such a way as to discourage the street slime from touching live metal surfaces. According to Mr. Drew, if this is done properly, whenever any unauthorized person touches the door handles, bumper, or hood latch, he will receive a jolt of electricity that feels like a right cross to the genitals. A small toggle switch located beneath the car will shut off the electricity whenever you wish.

I also got a lot of auto-related letters from people who are furious with the idiotic way drivers behave in shopping center parking lots. I agree. Parking in handicapped zones, fire lanes, walkways, and in front of stores is boorish, lazy, inconsiderate, and downright deserving of all sorts of Haydukian mayhem.

Pud Drunchniak tells me that he cruises the mall lots until he spots a repeat offender he has noted from before. Pud is retired, you see, and has a lot of time to help make our world more civilized.

"I see these uncivilized, healthy louts parked where they shouldn't be while some senior citizen or mother with her little kids has to hike through a hundred yards of slush from her spot in the parking lot to get to the store. That isn't right, and I do something about it."

Old vigilante Pud carries a Crossman air pistol and a WHAMO wrist rocket with an ample supply of ammo for both in his car. He parks with a clear shot at the offending vehicle well within range and fires several rounds at the vehicle, wounding its windows or finish.

"I wait until there is noise or something else distracting before I take action, of course," Pud advises. "Sometimes I work only at night. I make two or three attacks on different targets from different locations and positions, then I leave the mall for the day.

Once in awhile I work from the mall roof, too. But, I'm not as young and mobile as I used to be, so I mostly stick with my car."

That spring-loaded prick punch that machinists use is a handy pocket tool and quite aptly named for dealing with marks. With reasonable quietness, it will punch a few neat holes in the body panels of the mark's car, showing him where you think he should mount a few do-dads from Western Auto, or so says Texas's R.W.

Here's one that almost seems timid, as if the meek really have taken over the earth. It's another variation on how to get back at some lout who bangs his car door into your car at some parking facility. You just stick toothpicks in any and all locks on the mark's car, then break them off in the lock. It helps if it's winter and the toothpick is wet. Actually, this stunt will work in almost any lock.

Jimi the Z doesn't believe in just slashing tires. He says to use pliers and pull out the stems. But, he tells you to leave the stems there as it is a riot to watch marks try to stuff them back in. Jimi suggests this great payback for subhuman slimeballs, e.g., those rude bastards who steal handicapped parking spots.

Meanwhile, moving inside the vehicle, you've heard of bees in your bonnet? With apologies to our British cousins, David Muridae has a little surprise for your mark's automobile glove box. Our Illinois-based trickster suggests loosing a container full of bees or wasps into the glove box. The poor mark will bumble into that lot and learn what a sting operation is really like.

California's infamous Arlo Jones has a lot of splendid suggestions to help you modify your mark's automobile. For instance, if your mark's vehicle has power seats, move the seat into a totally uncomfortable position, then cut the power cable that controls movement, or superglue the control knob.

According to Arlo, you can also easily create an ant farm on wheels with the mark's car by removing the ashtrays in the rear seat armrests. You'll find a lot of space under there for you to stuff half-eaten hamburgers or roadkill, then dump a can of soda on that mess. You could also produce the start of an ant culture by picking up a few strays from the sidewalk and introducing them to their new home. Replace the ashtray and wait. Arlo also mentions that if your mark's car features hidden windshield wipers, removing them will create quite a shock next time your mark is out driving in the rain or snow.

If you like syringes of all sizes, Filthy McNasty, our resident expert on various forms of antiestablishment guerrilla warefare, also has some tactics to try on your mark's car. He says to fill a basting syringe with castor oil, then squirt it into the tailpipe and muffler of the mark's car. After a few minutes on the road, the vehicle will start to smoke beyond belief.

You can also use this syringe to squirt a good dose of formaldehyde, el tacko perfume, vile urine, or whatever else through the mark's car's open window. Or, crack the window, run a garden hose in, and flood his car for real.

Jimi the Z is full of more ideas. This time he wants to reprogram the mark's custom car horn—the type where the owner records his own tune onto the little keyboard or cassette recorder. Here's the new idea. Substitute some of your really gross stuff for his original selection. For example, among some Latins, the familiar refrain "Shave and a Haircut, Two Bits," is interpreted as meaning, "Screw Your Mother." This meaning was independently confirmed by an East L.A. friend of mine.

I surely brought out all the experts of the automobile sabotage trade. Jerald Jordan adds an improvement to the old trick of supergluing car locks by telling us that you can also use that famous glue to seal the door's weather stripping to the car body. Just apply the glue all the way around and slam the door.

If you'd like the police to stop his car and speak with your mark, you can attract their attention by disconnecting his rear turn signal lights or his rear car lights. Sam from Connecticut did this to a habitually drunken fellow employee who was a menace on the road. Sam wanted the police to nail him for drunk driving. He got police attention by removing the bulbs from the aforementioned drunk's car lights, causing police to pull the heavily marinated mark over. Result: a free trip to jail for the sot, plus a heavy fine.

Banks

The First Federalism Savings and Mistrust Bank of Reagan Wattles, Kansas, opened its records to local law enforcement types who wanted to make a case on a peace-loving resident who smoked dope, went his own way, and didn't think Right. The local oinkers were on a financial fishing trip, looking for any possible scrap of illegal something or other to trip up Our Hero. But he was clean.

To gain some revenge, Our Hero planned this one to happen while he was out of town on business (yes, he had a real job). He had a trusted lady from another town rent a safe deposit box under the name of one of the local policemen. She placed a loudly ticking, eight-day clock in a box. In another branch bank, she did the same thing and planted a tiny tape player set to run for three half-hour intervals each day. The batteries would power it for three weeks. On an endless loop tape she had a voice screaming in panic, "Help, help, this bank is holding me prisoner. I'm trapped behind this wall in a cell. Oh God, help me."

Our officer friend nearly lost his badge over this one . . . .

When Bob Grain was in business, a flaky school teacher wrote him a bad check. He submitted the check again, and it was paid. However, since this jerk was not high on anyone's list of favorite people, Bob decided to give him something else to do besides bothering people with his bad checks.

"First I noted the name of his bank and his account number," Bob reports. "Then, for the next several weeks, every time I got the opportunity, I'd drive by the after hours bank depository, fill out a blank deposit form with all his info, and deposit a penny in his account for him. After eight or ten one-cent deposits, the bank got all bent out of shape with him and called to see what he was trying to achieve by making their employees waste time crediting him with penny after penny.

"The school teacher was very apologetic to the bank but couldn't figure out an easy way to stop it since he wasn't doing it. When the penny deposits continued, the bank called him back and offered him two choices: take his Mickey Mouse account to some other bank, or change his account number and have new checks printed. By now he was highly indignant with the bank and told *them* to shove it. He is now banking elsewhere.

"From personal business experience I also learned this rather valuable trick," Bob reports. "Suppose you have forwarded a check for collection, and it bounces. It comes back marked to indicate the account did not have sufficient funds to pay that check. In all probability, that account is still open and has some funds remaining . . . just not enough to cover the check.

"If you trust Mr. Check Bouncer to eventually make good on his draft, the most prudent action is obviously to resubmit the check, hoping by the time it goes through the collection department the second time, he will have made a new deposit. But there are times when it might be more advantageous to 'eat' a portion of the money involved and settle for a lesser amount . . . but get something for sure.

"Banks are very shy about giving out the amount of money actually in a customer's account. A little detective work can sometimes reveal what you need to know. Let's suppose the check you're holding is for $1,000. You know Bouncer probably doesn't have that much in the account. Call the bank, tell them you are holding a check from Check Bouncer for $1,000 and give them his account number. Ask them to verify that he does have funds to cover the check. In a few minutes, they'll probably inform you that he doesn't. Thank them and tell them you won't take his check. Give it a few minutes and have a friend call back, and give another commercial name. Tell them Bouncer just wrote you a check for $700 and go through the whole procedure again. Let's suppose this time the word is that Bouncer's account can cover the check. Thank them.

"Now you have two numbers with a $300 spread. You know he has at least $700, but not as much as $1,000. Give it a few more minutes; the chances of getting a different employee are pretty good in large banks. Call back; this time ask about an $800 check . . . 'Yes,' they say, 'there are sufficient funds.' Thank them again. You know it's over $800 and less than $1,000.

"Call 'em back and try $900 on them, same ruse. Let's suppose this time the word is 'No.' At this point, you probably know more about Bouncer's account than he does. And, there is a way to recover a substantial amount of that $1,000.

"You know his account number and name and address from his check. Drive to the bank and try for a drive-in teller. Pick up a blank deposit slip on the way. You've narrowed it down to a $200 spread, so use your own money to make a $200 cash deposit in Bouncer's account and ask the teller to credit it promptly, acting as if you are Bouncer, and tell her you're afraid you're going to be overdrawn. That should get the $200 credited immediately.

"Make a bee-line for the front door and present Bouncer's $1,000 check for collection. If everything goes as it should, they should pay off the check, leaving his account almost empty. You recovered $800 from his account. If he actually had $850, you ended up leaving him an extra $50, so you really lost $250 on this jerk . . . but you didn't take the chance of losing the full kilobuck," Bob advises.

"What's really upsetting is that banks are so scuzzy that if you just walk in the front door and present the $1,000 check without all this advance work, they will probably decline payment. If you tell them you'll accept any monies in his account, in lieu of full payment, they will protect this scumbag and themselves and still decline payment. Then, while you're walking away, the next person may present another of Bouncer's checks, this time for $850 and have it paid immediately, no questions asked."

Bob also tells us that many computerized bank deposit programs give you a printout showing the new balance. This way, say, if you were depositing a dime or so in your mark's account, you would also learn his or her total balance. This bit of information is wonderful to know, both for your use and for prevention of use by your enemies. Gee, just sitting there reading Bob's letter, I thought of five or six rotten uses for this information.

Bars

A lot of women won't go into bars alone because derelicts of all persuasions will bug them. Some guys report that these creeps hit on their dates even with them present. What's this world coming to? Anyway, one young lady found a scam to strike back at these score-artists. Her name is Wanda Woodland, and here's her method.

"I like to have a few drinks without all sorts of creeps bothering me. But, it never works out that way. I decided to make them as miserable as they made me. So, one night, I let a guy buy me all kinds of drinks, and I ordered the most expensive stuff I could get. We then went through the 'ride home' ritual of stopping at a cocktail lounge with a motel. I had insisted we take my car which was O.K. with him. He didn't know it, but it was essential for my plan.

"His line was offered and I accepted. So far, I hadn't even had to kiss the jerk, and he hadn't tried to touch me. I let him pay for the motel room, and while he was in the shower getting all sexy, I took out my lipstick and wrote on the large mirror above the bed, "MY FUN WAS IN YOUR CHASE . . . START WITHOUT ME," quietly left the room, got in my car, and went home . . . laughing all the way."

Bathrooms

Hedley Herndon from L.A. has a good idea for any mark who displays an anal personality. He claims that he invited a guy to several parties and the man made a complete ass of himself with the ladies, food, and drink. Hedley thought payback was in order. He quietly walked into one of the mark's drunken parties and found a spare roll of toilet paper in the closet.

"I had some Tabasco sauce in a small spray bottle. I didn't want to hurt anyone at the party, so I unrolled some of the paper on the spare roll, then sprayed a few feet of it, let it dry, then rolled it back up again and put it back for him alone to use," Hedley relates.

BB Machine Gun

That BB machine gun sold via mail by a specialty outfit down in Florida, is a formidable glass-trashing device. When I think of BB guns and glass, I usually think in terms of small pockmarks. But, that's what happens when you do a number on a window with a Daisy. The air-fed machine gun variety is a whole different ball game. The steady stream of BBs does unbelievable damage. At a range of four feet, on a two second drive-by, a reader put a hundred BBs into the side windows of his mark's parked car. He trashed all four side windows in several seconds, and the glass just fell out in what he described as "an ice-maker gone berserk." The glass just collapsed under the steady impact.

These guns use a can of automobile air conditioning freon for the propellent. With a little customizing, they can be hooked up to a compressed air bottle as well. In this particular incident, the car was a company auto—the boss's car—being used by the mark without his permission while he was out of town. The object of the sneak attack was simply to create a need for the mark to explain it all to his boss.

Billboards

Check the *Graffiti* section, too, but for this chapter, I'm indebted to Gordon Goofbutt of Friendship, Maryland, for persuading some of his colleagues to do some creative captioning on local billboards. After painting over the existing advertising headlines, they inserted their own balloon/caption combinations. Gordon says most were gross and obscene, e.g., on one billboard showing a handsome couple smoking a well-known cigarette brand, the male is saying to the female, "Sit on my face, and I'll guess your weight."

Bounty Hunters

Look through the dozens of relatively recent "Wanted" posters in the post office for some nasty criminal who looks like your mark. Hopefully, your mark is not too well known or is a newcomer. According to J. Edgar Murtha, it's amazingly true that in checking two hundred or so posters you'll be able to come up with six people who have a fairly close resemblance to your various enemies or marks. Borrow these posters.

To put this plan into action, show your mark's poster (or use Xerox copies to which you've affixed a seal from your notary stamp—described in earlier books) around macho bars where amateur bounty hunters and other guys who read *Soldier of Fortune* hang out. Drop word that you're a pro hunter and that there's a $25,000 reward for this person. In hard times your wanted poster, and your mark, will attract a lot of attention. If you're especially ballsy, visit the local constables and show them the poster copies.

The thing that really makes this work, according to Murtha, is *also* showing some realistic stakeout-type photos of the subject which you have taken yourself. Explain that these are "surveillance" photos. Let your bounty hunter or constable compare the photos and the poster. The closer you get to the mark's neighborhood, the faster your operation will come home to haunt him.

Bureaucrats

Bubba Bates was had by a buck-passing bureaucrat in Florida, i.e., he was screwed out of a good job by this paperwork parasite. Buck had an advertising inspiration. He placed an ad in local papers offering jobs to "Male Secretaries Only." He included such come-ons in the copy as "$11 an hour, must be physically attractive and gentle," plus a few more choice character traits. He then listed the mark's name and office location with a strong "no phone calls" admonition in the ad. He set the show-up-for-interview time as one half-hour prior to the mark's office actually opening. That meant that when the bureaucratic mark arrived at work on the morning in question, he had a lot of very ungentle male secretaries bitching away at each other and then at him for his cattle call style of recruitment. I'd be willing to bet that some members of the local vice squad were there, too. Bubba Bates says you can repeat this one as often and with as many variations as you feel the mark requires.

Business Reply Mail

A few weeks ago I got some unwanted mail trying to raise funds to buy private military supplies for one or more of the fascist dictatorships in Latin America. I have little time for these enemies of all free people, so I thought I would donate some medical supplies . . . collect . . . as there was a return reply envelope included with their mailing.

Using a tactic borrowed from a right-wing acquaintance, I got several old gasoline cans and filled them with used oil . . . perfect for treating skin problems like redass and redneck. I packaged them well and marked the parcel EMERGENCY MEDICAL SUPPLIES . . . PRIORITY MAIL. I put their postage-paid return envelope on the parcel and mailed it. The good old USPS took care of it very handily for me, even with a smile. Maybe that's because I was smiling, too.

Candy

Every home or office has candy thieves . . . the folks who say, "Oh, I really shouldn't but . . . ." The worst ones, though, are those silent sneakers who empty your candy box while your back is turned. Here is a little appetizer for them. Collect dead insects from dusty window sills. Cover the little corpses with chocolate and put them in with the real candy. Bon appetit.

This one may take some getting used to, and you may not even want to read it . . . it's pretty yukky. But, it came in and is sworn to as true by the perpetrator. It shows me how far people will go when they are frustrated or screwed over by someone else. Our source here is a man who wants to call himself The Phantom from Whitman's Samplers. You'll see the cogency in a moment.

Mr. Phantom got fired without cause by his very rotten boss, but only after the young employee had set up a system of accounting which would save the company a lot of money. After the employee set up the system and explained it, the boss fired him and turned it over to his wife to operate. Wives don't have to be paid, I guess.

Mr. Phantom's revenge was, ahh, sweet. Here's his story.

"My ex-boss was having a party for some of his equally crass friends. I decided to send along a present of my own 'homemade candy' which I had an ally, a friendly bartender, slip into the party.

I made sure my present was all done up nicely in a Whitman Sampler box with real candy. Here's how I prepared that gift.

"Several nights before the party I ate six ears of corn for dinner . . . nothing else. Later that evening, I ate two apples (a great source of pectin). The next morning I moved my bowels into a plastic bag. I allowed the feces to dry in the sun for two days. Wearing rubber gloves, I cut that dried block into small squares the size of cherries. They were semihard with whole kernels of corn running through them, a decidedly disgusting visual effect.

"Then, I melted four large bars of milk chocolate in a double boiler, and, not unlike a fondue, I gently covered the feces pieces with the delectable milk chocolate.

"When they were dry, I wrapped each one in the golden foil that the original chocolate-covered cherries come wrapped in. I filled the box and resealed it."

According to Mr. Phantom, the bartender said the "gift" was devoured for a few moments until one guest finally spit out a piece of "candy." Within two minutes, there was not enough bathroom space to accommodate eighteen gastrically ill guests involuntarily intent upon regurgitating.

Cassette Tapes

   Our ubiquitous Jimi the Z has a stunt for matron/marks and
other lovers of Lawrence Welk, 101 Strings, Frank Sinatra, and
other geeks like those. Of course, their musical taste isn't what
makes them marks. You are merely using that taste to hit back.
Jimi says to get access to their favorite tapes and record over their
numbers with rotten selections by Frank Zappa, the Sex Pistols,
or Captain Beefheart.

CBs

CB must be a dying species. As I drive across our country on the potholed mazes we used to call highways, I rarely hear the Good Buddies like I used to a few years ago. Nonetheless, if you are still bothered by a troublesome CBer, beg, borrow, or buy with full-intent-to-return the biggest, most powerful linear amplifier you can locate that will work with your mobile CB. Pull up in your mark's driveway or near his vehicle when you know he is on the air. Wait until he is receiving, then key down with all the power your unit can muster. Poof! You put him off the air, and maybe, through the roof.

If your mark has graduated from CB to ham radio, and you can get his license call letters and access to a radio to use, you can have a lot of fun. Play funky and kinky music, jam out repeaters and simplex operations, keep giving his call sign over the air, talk dirty, and then cursingly dare other ham operators to track you down. Abuse them verbally. Abuse their mothers. CAUTION: stay mobile and be prepared to move fast, fast, fast. Hams are the best signal trackers anywhere—far better than the FCC or those Nazis you always see using radio tracking vans to hunt down spies and resistance leaders in WWII movies. All this expert technical advice comes from Filthy McNasty, who knows because he does.

Chemicals

Dr. Doyle Conan, our medical adviser, said to mention gentian violet as a great helper. Officially, it is a powdered substance used for washing laboratory slides. But a problematic side effect is that it stains the skin a rich shade of deep purple and is nearly impossible to wash off. According to Dr. Conan, it takes a week of repeated scrubbing to remove the stain.

"The stuff is nontoxic, so you can put it in a spraying device to annoint offending animals, children, ex-lovers, etc.," Dr. Conan claims.

Conjuring up an old experience from the Hayduke Depository of Rotten Things I've Done to Deserving Folks, a friend and I had gotten some gentian violet one summer and sprinkled the powder on some snooty bitches as they lay sunning their vain bodies around a country club swimming pool. A combination of perspiration, oil, and heat caused the powder to stick. As the light staining began, the young ladies raced to the pool to wash off the offending and spreading color. I leave the rest to your imagination.

You remember the book *Black, Like Me?* Credit silver nitrate, also known as lunar caustic, for the ability to blacken one's skin. According to the Rev. J. Richard Young, one ounce of this in a standard bottle of suntan oil will cause the mark's afflicted parts to turn quite black for several days. It is also highly soluble in warm water, which can be sprayed.

I once knew a hospital orderly in the service who used it on a truly racist soldier whose waking moments were spent cursing blacks. The orderly gave the bigot a sponge bath with a solution containing a good dose of silver nitrate. In a day the man's color went from Redneck to Ethnic Dark. A nurse in on the gag told him that his last blood transfusion had been donated by a soldier of the Negro persuasion. It never changed the bigot's mentality, but it surely blew his mind for a few days.

Another reader who used silver nitrate was Marie from New Orleans, who said she mixed it into some shaving cream owned by a friend who had done her an injustice. It worked just fine, as she reports with a chuckle about his unwanted man tan.

A nasty chemical known as copper sulfate is deadly poisonous to aquatic life, as any sportsman knows. Farmers know it is also very injurious to trees. If, for some ungodly reason, you want to kill someone's aquatic life or trees, this stuff will do the trick. Two pounds dumped into a pond will do the job, while four ounces poured around the drip line—the outer edge of the leaves of any given tree—will murder the tree. Personally, I'd rather hurt people than fish or trees.

The canny Rev. J. Richard Young offers a fantastic tear gas substitute for nasty dogs, cats, rats, bats, kids, and for use during domestic spats. Go to a chemical supply house and buy Formaldehyde 97%. Tell them you or your kid has a big insect collection or something. Put it in a nasal spray bottle and fire away. It will temporarily knock the socks off anything hit in the face with it.

It's no lie, says Herb Bobwander, that lye is a great tool for the trickster. Herb suggests you wrap some lye in a newspaper, fasten it with rubber bands, then drop or throw this projectile onto your mark's car roof, roof gutters, or other areas you want to be eaten through. The lye will ruin paint, eat holes in soft metals, plus stain paint, and kill vegetation. Now that's what I call the right stuff.

Christmas Trees

Stoney Dale used to live two doors away from a cantankerous old man who never had a kind word for anyone. The man verbally abused his neighbors and their kids and pets, took potshots with a BB gun, or was always calling the police for things he imagined people were doing to him. The police regarded him as a crank and dreaded his calls. Stoney took it upon himself to get even on behalf of the suffering neighborhood.

"Two days past Christmas I ran an ad in the local paper, saying, 'I have a need for all evergreen trees used for Christmas decoration. Please leave them on my driveway or lawn. I will pay you $3 per tree.' I used the old grump's name and address with the ad. The newspaper took my cash and never checked the story. Within two days the old man's property was buried with the remains of the town's Yuletide," Stoney relates.

College Life

Jim Klann has a check-bouncing idea that he used to pull on slobs and others who did rotten things to him while he was working his way through college. It was relatively simple, and it will work on almost any mark, not just college students, in lots of situations.

"I would place a call to the mark, identify myself as the college bursar and inform him that his last tuition check had just bounced. If it was his check, that was it. If it was his parents' check, I told him to call home immediately.

"I always called about three minutes before five o'clock so that if he asked for more details like the amount or check number, I could mumble something about the file clerk already locking up the records and that the office was closing. Then, I'd get stern again and tell him to call us back first thing in the morning."

Jim's scam had the mark calling home and worrying all night about bouncing a check, owing service fees, and good stuff like that.

Irritated because some mature and outstanding young men who belonged to the right social fraternity at the University of Illinois stole, molested, and terrorized his date, then threw up on his car, a fellow student who was majoring in Haydukery came up a winner. There was an outdoor beer party at the fraternity that afternoon. Our man had another student walk over and tell the frat guys that some students from another campus were going to try to crash the party that afternoon, only they'd be dressed as local cops. Then, later, our hero called the local cops to complain about the lawn party.

Later, this same student was awakened one morning by a crew of surly construction workers from another town. They were busily and noisily digging up the sidewalk in front of his room. It was 6:08. He dressed and went to his eight o'clock class early. On his way out, he stopped and talked with a couple of the workers. He told them that the last time a crew worked near campus, a bunch of fraternity guys dressed up as campus cops tried to hassle the workers as a practical joke. The workers didn't like this idea one bit.

Later, just before going into his class, our agitator called the campus police office and told them a bunch of fraternity guys were dressed up as a construction crew and were digging up the sidewalk at such and such an address. When they asked him who he was, he gave them the name of the president of the fraternity mentioned earlier.

Aren't you sorry you didn't go to school with Joe from New Orleans? He's the guy who epoxy'd shut a deserving mark's dorm room door the night before the kid's most important final exams. Why did Joe do this?

"He (the mark) was a badass, always coming in drunk and blowing his dinner on us, after a beer party; you know, throwing up in our rooms. Nothing nice to correct him worked, so we figured if we made him miss his finals, he'd flunk the courses and be out of school."

In another case, one of Joe's dormmates from another floor used to think it was great fun to turn in false fire alarms. That costs everyone something and is a stupid thing to do. Joe didn't think it was too funny either. He got several surplus fire extinguishers on the sly from a sympathetic fireman friend, and they filled the mark-who-cried-fire's room with foam while the kid lay in a drunken stupor.

If you thought Joe was nasty, try Kevin from the same grand old city over there in Louisiana. His mark was a bully who was always doing nasty things to nice people. Kevin gave him a double-barreled dose of his own meanness. He waited until the mark boldly announced he was going to cut a few days of classes to go shack up with some campus tootsie he'd picked up in a bar. Kevin then called the school administration and each of the mark's teachers and told them that he (Kevin) was the undertaker (using a real name) from the mark's hometown and that the kid had died suddenly and to please take him off the class lists, enrollment files, and the master computer list. He said a letter and death certificate would follow by mail. Then, Kevin's buddy posed as a school official, called the mark's parents and told them their son was dead as a result of a party prank. Kevin never went near the mark again. A lot of other people did though, and the mark had a lot of explaining to do.

Wouldn't it be neat to get a bunch of course withdrawal forms from some office on campus and fill them out in your mark's name? You could then feed them to the computer through the appropriate clerk and have the mark officially withdrawn from classes. The poor mark, of course, will continue to go to class, take tests, do assignments, worry about grades, and all that good stuff. Only at the end of the term will he or she realize what happened.

Computers

To err is human, but to really muck up things requires a computer. That's the good word from Jim Whitehead, our computer expert. According to Jim, any competent programmer on a medium or large computer can write a program that generates another program and so on. You have the original program generate two others, each with different random names. These programs are copies of the original.

Thus, an electronic "tumor" will be created which doubles every half hour or so, eventually bringing the entire system to a grinding halt. Jim says you can also bury this tumor in a program, to be activated only when a certain set of conditions happen, creating a computer time bomb.

One of Jim's other refinements could make merry times for someone in corporatedom. He notes that some systems are so computerized that they generate, write, and mail letters automatically without having a human involved. It's all in the programming. Jim leaves it to the imagination of each reader to devise uses for this ability, e.g., use the computer to sign the names of uptight officers of a very straight corporation on letters advocating a satanic cult to be sent to stockholders. Use the corporate letterhead, of course.

Not one to ignore upgrading treachery along with the establishment's technology, may I offer a new piece of equipment for use in confusing computers. Computer expert Gunther Girkin says that large magnets aren't very efficient at upsetting computers and suggests the use of an E-Bow. An E-Bow is a little gizmo that electric guitar players use to get that "Wah-Wah" sound. It sets up an AC magnetic field to vibrate the guitar strings. Girkin says that same field does a helluva job on computer tapes, floppies, hard discs, etc. One big drawback is that an E-Bow costs over a hundred dollars. Of course, you could get friendly with a guitar player and borrow one for your attack.

Condoms

Big Jules Torquato of Newark came up with a piercing twist to the old idea of sticking holes in condoms. It seems his sister was living with her supposedly faithful sweetheart. Then, one day little sister found a hefty supply of Trojans. She thought this a bit odd since she was on the pill. Then she recalled the late nights, the early mornings, the excuses, the odd odors, and other things about her lover's behavior of late that didn't add up—until she found the hidden condoms.

Jules' sister put the venerable pin pricks in the rubber goods, then put them back carefully so that Mr. Wrong would continue to rely on their effectiveness. When Jules found out about all of this, he added the final touch (ouch!). He carefully skewered a large pin into the last condom, as a signal that its owner had misplaced his trust in his organ as much as Jules' little sister had in him.

Convenience Stores

If you'd like to add a secondary mark to your revenge on a guilty convenience store, enjoy this idea sent along by Sam Stein, a Connecticut Hayduker with a great sense of humor. Sam says to call the store and have them set aside about ten copies of today's newspaper and hold them for _____ (secondary mark's name). If the papers arrive at 2:00 P.M., call about 3:30, as this will give them time to sell most copies and be down to the last ones for rush-hour traffic commuters. In any case, when you gather your intelligence, note numbers of papers and times sold so you are sure to reserve the last copies.

You tell the clerk that you'll pick up your copies within the hour as you're coming from work. By 5:30, the salesclerk usually calls the mark's home. If he or she is home, the clerk may complain, but, usually, they'll get things straightened out. If the mark's not home, it works even better.

Call the clerk back about 6:30 and say you were delayed in traffic and are still intending to pick up the newspapers. Tell the clerk you'll be there by 7:00. The clerk will probably raise hell. Try innocence. Blame "your brother" for answering your phone at home, playing a joke on him/her, and of course you want the papers. Be adamant.

Call the store at 7:30 and tell the clerk you don't want the papers anymore because the news is all old. The clerk will really raise hell now. You should get abusive. Repeat who is calling. Use the mark's name often and threaten the clerk.

Other things you can tell the clerk are that you'll trash the store, burn it down, burn his or her car, or torture him/her. If the clerk threatens to call the police, tell him to go ahead and try. Say you'll be down there in three minutes to kill him *and* the "gawdamn pig-cops."

Within moments, the police will be rushing Code 3 to your mark's home in swarms with all lights and sirens blaring. Sam says that if the cops don't show because the clerk failed to call, then visit the store that night and toss a brick through the window or dump the mark's garbage in the store or on the sidewalk (see *Garbage*). Then, start the entire process over again.

Credit Cards

Gennifer Roberta Glotinis, our credit card wizard, lets you know how truly easy it is to cancel your mark's credit card. You simply call the company telephone number and give them the mark's name and address. You don't need the card number, but it would give you lots more credibility if you could provide it. Ms. Glotinis tells me this scam works and sometimes they don't even check on such claims before taking action. As an alternative, report your mark's card as lost or stolen.

Delicatessens

The only bad thing about The Clay Demolay Delicatessen is the fact that bugs, insects, and other many-legged vermin are among its best customers. While the employees begged for sanitation improvements, the owner, Myers Demolay, just chortled and counted his profits. One of these employees, whom we'll call Deliboy Dave, finally tired of begging for better working conditions. He decided to bug the boss, literally.

"One summer, we had a mammoth order for hoagies that I had to prepare. The big horse flies were buzzing all around as I worked," Deliboy Dave recounts, "so, I started using two pieces of provolone cheese as a compression fly swatter. I'd blast a few bugs between the two slices of cheese, leaving the small corpses and attendant gore on the slices.

"Then, I'd add the fly 'n' guts garnished slices to the hoagies on our assembly line. Nobody noticed, and about one hundred-fifty hoagies went out that day. I didn't work the next day, but I was told that some eighty irate people stormed the place."

Department Stores

Mike Leary was a strange enough guy but a victim of his own circumstances, i.e., he was lazy and thus, difficult to employ. It was under this cloud that he was browsing in the Lou A. Miller House of Fashion one spring day. He was daydream shopping for his nonexistent girlfriend when a clerk asked if she might help him. He smiled and said he was just looking. She frosted him with a glance and went to search for the manager.

Mrs. Miller personally told Mr. Leary that he should not loiter in her store unless he was a serious customer. At that point, Mr. Leary grew very serious intentions in his mind. He left the store right away. He made plans over the next few weeks, including recon and buying some supplies. Then, on the big day, he shaved, put on his best suit, and went back into the store just before closing time.

He waited carefully a few moments, then ducked quietly into a dressing stall on the floor. He knew that the clerks never checked there before locking up at night since he had done his intelligence recon before pulling his stunt. When the last person had left, Mr. Leary brought out his bag of tricks.

He went quickly to the display window and started giving the mannequins some fashion accessories in the most appropriate places. For example, on an elegant lady mannequin, he placed a chewed cigar butt in her upraised fingers. In the hand of another female mannequin, he hung a dripping douche bag. A male dummy was now posed with the business end of an enema fixture in his one hand. The tube disappeared elsewhere. Let me give you a list of some of the other objects that Mr. Leary placed with the window and in-store mannequins in his brief fifteen minutes of action before he quietly and safely left the store. They included: three large dildoes, a squash, a pizza, two accu-jac devices, two vinyl female sex dolls, an Elvis poster, and some plastic religious artifacts. You can play mix-and-match to figure what went where.

Dial-A-Joke

Joe Copcheck's old uncle was bamboozled by a fast-talking salesman for a publishing firm and ended up with a dozen unwanted book and magazine subscriptions. Reasonable, orderly, and rational letters didn't help the old man in his attempts to return the books, nor did Joe's telephone calls on his uncle's behalf. So, they decided not to pay anymore, hoping to hear from an understanding human. Instead, the elderly man was bugged night and day by the publisher's sales rep's bullying phone calls, then by threats of collection agencies, and finally, by the dunning agents themselves. All of this was for a $200 balance on a $350 unwanted order which he had tried to cancel. Joe finally got angry enough to do something outside the line of reason. But, he kept his sense of humor.

"Every city has a Dial-A-Joke line. You can never get through because the line is always tied up by someone else calling . . . all hours of the day and night," Joe informs me. "I used $200 of my own money—the same amount the bastards were terrorizing my uncle for—and placed ads in some local newspapers, including the local college paper, for a 'Brand New Off-The-Wall Dial-A-Joke Service. ADULTS ONLY!'

"Obviously, I listed the publishing house's various office telephone numbers. Then, through a friend who works for the phone company, I got the unlisted home telephone numbers of the publisher and the president of the collection agency. I ran these numbers with an ad in a local scuzzy porno sheet offering "Free Sex Calls! Our Hot, Young Coeds Play with Themselves and Talk Dirty to You—All Free to Introduce Our New Service! CALL TODAY!"

Joe and his uncle had their money's worth and eventually, the company and collection agency gave up, as Joe knew they would, because it didn't pay to take the old man to court for $200. So, the Copchecks got a lot of laughs besides the books and magazines.

Joe also passes along some variations of this scam, e.g., Dial-A-Prayer for an atheistic mark; Dial-A-Nazi for a Jewish mark, or vice-versa; and Dial-An-Orgasm for a prudish mark. Advertise in local papers or post handbills and enjoy the fun. Joe asks only that you keep those calls a'coming, gang.

Dirty Old (and Young) Men

It seems as if college kids have all the fun. Actually, for every person having the fun, there is probably a victim who needs to fight back. For example, John and Dave were roommates at the University of Virginia in Charlottesville. I know the place well, as a young lady and I were once apprehended there in a condition of being drunk and very disorderly by local police. But, that was years ago. Recently, Dave complained because he was always getting kicked out of their room by John. The reason was that John was one of the top dirty young men on campus. There have probably been more women in his bed than springs in his mattress.

Not having the same luck or problem, and needing to study and sleep, Dave spoke with John about some consideration. John said he was on a roll, so to speak, and the hell with his roomie. Dave enlisted the help of his friend Jim, the computer expert, and they got even.

Jim says, "We took the thin foil of an empty condom wrapper and placed it in the middle of a deck of John's computer class cards that he was ready to run through the machine.

"About an hour or so after he submitted his program (the cards), John got a call to report immediately to the office of the Computer Systems administrator. Leaning over his massive desk, this fat, red-faced bureaucrat hissed at John, 'It took us nearly an hour to dig this (holding up the condom foil) out of our card reader. You cost us over $500 in down time. You must think you're pretty damn smart . . . '

"John was totally taken aback. He stammered and stuttered some kind of apology and was told, 'We won't forget this and neither will your reputation.' John soon became known as The Condom Kid, and because of all this, girls started to shun him. Dave soon got his half of the room back again."

This gag works both on dirty old men (DOM) *and* dirty young men (DYM).

A lot of people ask what they can do to put down the DOM supervisors who figure sexual harassment will work in a pinch during our hard economic times. One reader had an answer. She worked in state government and her slimeball boss told her it was either put out or get out. Instead, she got him put out.

"I got hold of the man's resume through another lady who was personally sympathetic because she'd been down that road with him before. I made copies of the resume and sent them all over the place to other state government offices with a personal cover letter 'from' my supervisor/mark. I explained that 'I' wanted a transfer because 'my' boss was making homosexual advances toward 'me.'

"You can imagine the impact when word filtered back to the mark's boss about these letters 'from' my supervisor. My boss was shaken and shattered when his boss confronted him. No amount of explaining and denying could straighten out the ill feeling.

"Finally, I had both a male friend and another girl friend call the supervisor at home and tell him that he hadn't seen anything yet unless he stopped his shabby, sexual harassment of women. He did."

Don't cross the Claw of Justice, as one reader from British Columbia calls himself. He had a dirty old man bothering a lady friend of his and the creep wouldn't take "get lost" for an answer. The Claw and his friend found out that all mail addressed to individuals at the DOM's corporate office was opened by mail clerks and routed from there. The next step was obvious. They designed and had printed some disgusting letterhead and envelopes for a magazine named *Gay Bondage*. They wrote the mark, in care of his employer, telling him "we're sorry, the women's leather undergarments you ordered in a men's large size have been delayed in shipment."

Later, when it was time for the office Christmas party, our friends sent him a pair of perfumed black bikini underwear, soaked in sickening perfume, with a note that read, "You loved taking these off me when you had me on your office desk. Smell them and reconsider your decision not to see me again . . . Love, Celeste." The Claw says you can also send that last one to the mark's home for his prune-faced wife to enjoy with him during the holiday season . . . or whenever.

Drugs

Everyone who smokes a bit of dope gets hit on by moochers. Wayne Weed from New Orleans has one way of dealing with chronic or obnoxious moochers. "Hey, I'm as generous as they come, to a point. After a while, forget it, man. What I do is roll some joints using parsley and maybe a few dead seeds scattered in for realism. Serious dopers get the message soon, others don't. What's funny is the amateurs who think they're high . . . on parsley . . . that's the hilarious part," says Wayne.

Some sophisticates from L.A., namely Larry and someone signing his letter Zapata, suggest that you grind up a No-Doz pill or two and put it into a little envelope known in drug circles as a bindle. Use this as a plant, then do your duty as a good citizen to report the suspicious person, i.e., your mark, for possession.

Explosives

Pume sodium is banned from commercial aircraft because it becomes extremely reactive when it comes in contact with water in any form. Pume p osphorus, its neighbor, is also not allowed on aircraft because it will ignite spontaneously in air at temperatures about 85°F. These two facts are from the lessons of Dr. Foge Football, George Hayduke Professor of Chemistry at Zambotti University. They are for your personal use.

It is getting tougher and harder for decent, good, solid citizens to buy fireworks, either legally or otherwise. If it's tough for them, think what it is for the likes of you and me! That's where Filthy McNasty comes to our blow-it-yourself rescue.

Filthy wants you to try his recipe for making your own M-80s to be used in various gags. He says this is the best method he ever heard of and believe me. Filthy is an expert.

"To make the M-80s, you need precut casing stock three-fourths of an inch inside diameter by half an inch inside diameter, the green style of M-80 safety fuse, potassium perchlorate, German black aluminum powder, half-inch end plugs, and glue," says Filthy.

"First, cut the casing stock into casings one and a half inches long. Plug one end with a half-inch end plug and glue. Allow to dry. Punch a one-eighth inch hole in the center of the side of the casing and insert a three-inch piece of safety fuse. Secure with a drop of glue and allow to dry. Repeat for as many casings as you want.

"Now it's time to mix the powder. In a coffee can, mix seven parts of potassium perchlorate and three parts of the German black aluminum powder. But, please wear some type of face mask and heavy gloves while doing this for your own safety.

"When you've mixed the two chemicals thoroughly, the powder is done. Keep it in the coffee can, covered, until needed. These parts are measured by grams, so a decent gram scale should be used. Get a good one it's worth it in the long run," Filthy adds.

"Fill each casing about three-quarters full with the powder and glue in the other end plug. Allow to dry. The finished M-80s can now be painted and waterproofed. To waterproof, simply rub some paraffin wax on the casing and the ends. This isn't really necessary but is a good idea."

These M-80s are really very powerful, so caution is advised. Enjoy!

All of these items are sold by Westech and are of excellent quality (see *Sources*).

A small amount of crushed iodine crystals is the starter for a fine contact explosive. According to the Rev. J. Richard Young, cover the crushed crystals with a few ounces of nondetergent household ammonia or use ammonium hydroxide. Let it all sit for ten minutes, then pour off the liquid. You must then store this crystal explosive in a well-stoppered vial out of sunlight and at a temperature below 100°F. Heat and sunlight cause rapid deterioration. According to the reverend, this will store actively for months in your freezer.

It is a noisy and relatively safe explosive. But, it must be dry to blow. For example, you could break off the graphite on the end of a pencil, then coat the pencil end with the explosive. When someone sharpens this pencil, there will be a BOOM. Dab a small amount on light switches, door knobs, or sprinkle it on floors. But use small amounts so nobody is physically injured. Damp or soiled pants we don't care about.

Fan Club Freaks

Sometimes fan club freaks are obnoxious, even dangerous. A radio station personality was actually assaulted by an Elvis freak because he wouldn't keep playing her favorite selections.

"I got back at her by puking a colorfully spectacular cascade of vomit from pizza, wine, carrots, and candy into a plastic bag a week later. I tossed in a whole bunch of vitamin capsules and other pills, then mailed it to her at work, telling her that the National Elvis Fan Club was donating this package of 'Elvis's Last Supper' to her."

Long live the King!

Fast Food Stores

Here's a switch. Suppose you work at one of these gastronomic whorehouses and want to get back at some of the absolute idiot customers who make your life awful. There are lots of people who stop at fast food shops and demand the world and everything else in the most obnoxious way. Want to pay them back . . . while still smiling?

- Freddie from San Antonio works at (don't you wish you knew?) and says when someone urinates him off, he coughs up huge wet hawkers and blows them into their food before serving it.
- Allen, who works in Boston, cools off his temper from dealing with an awful customer by walking into the cooler and placing pieces of used toilet paper between ground beef patties of a franchise favorite.
- Sid used to do worse when a customer upset him without reason where he cooked. He would actually dab little flecks of feces on their patties after he had cooked them.
- At nationally recognized franchises that feature fries, you'll think about Larry, the cook. If he is irritated the night before, without fail, the next morning he will pee into every French fry bin.

Perhaps Bob Grain was on the mark's end of one of these employee stunts. Maybe that's why he drove to his local fast food outlet that used an outdoor two-way "drive-in" order device. Bob says he ordered a huge, expensive, and complicated meal, then immediately drove on through the line and away, far away.

I asked one of my moles inside a local fast food mark about this. She said there was a very good chance that the people in the car behind Bob's would get the order. If it were a big, complicated order, there would be an argument. If it were small, they might pay for it before realizing something was wrong. Hopefully, by then, as Bob noted, their kids would have it scattered all over the car. Of such wonders are dreams made? My mole says the best time to pull this off would be the busy times at lunch and during evening meal hours. She says it will work.

May I take your order?

Fears

Most people fear the unknown. Dr. Paul Wilson, a noted psychic, says, "That old fear of the dark, of the bogeyman, of what lies under our beds at night is with us all to some extent or another." George W. Hayduke, Jr., a noted rotten person, says this universal fear can be used to your advantage against almost any mark.

Odd noises at night, strange lights and/or sounds, bizarre telephone calls, cult and occult pictures sent through the mail, someone staring at the mark . . . all sorts of things can be done to prey on the mark's insecurities. Fear belongs; use it wisely.

Flowers

Barbara from Chicago once lost her man to a true tramp. Using her mind rather than her body to fight back, Barbara sent this hussy a floral arrangement in the man's name. Included amid all the "ohh and ahh" pretty posies were selected portions of poison ivy.

Forgery

A lot of strange people call in when I'm on talk shows. One of them not only claimed to have spent time in the slammer for passing bad checks, but also said he was truly a professional forger. He passed along the advice that you can disguise your handwriting by wearing one or more pair of gloves when you want to write something in a handwriting other than your own, for whatever reason. While he was relating this I was wondering why, if he's so good, he was in prison!

Garage Door Openers

Many garage door openers work for more than one door. Usually, the cheaper the model, the more universal its application, according to our electronic entry expert, Toby Bill. He has a collection of openers, plus a friend who can modify a unit into a fairly universal electronic master key.

"We entertain ourselves by countermanding the legitimate use of openers by nasty neighbors, lowlifes, and other marks. Once, we had unusually good timing and managed to close a heavy double door in the middle of a Lincoln Continental our mark was backing out of his garage. Crunch! Other times, we open doors late at night in hopes vermin and varmints will infest the mark's living area."

Garbage

If my mail is any indicator, A.J. Weberman is not the only noted American garbologist. For example, The Night Lurker robs his mark's mailbox, removes only the junk mail, mixes it with various items of trash and garbage, then tosses them onto other people's lawns.

We can thank Stoney Dale for dragging out this tidbit of garbage. He had yet another grouchy neighbor who was hated by one and all. The man left for work at seven in the morning, while Stoney departed several hours later. In the meantime, the garbage truck made its rounds of the neighborhood. Stoney had a friend from another part of town stop by his house on garbage day, and here's what happened.

"Just as the garbage men pulled up in front of the Grinch's house, my friend would stroll down the mark's driveway like he lived there. He told the men that his wife had misplaced her watch and he was going to search the garbage for it. He told them not to worry about pickup," Stoney relates. "They didn't and soon left."

Stoney says the Grinch didn't say anything about his garbage bags being the only ones in evidence in the neighborhood that night. But when the following week rolled around, Grinch put out another set of bags. Stoney's pal pulled the same stunt. This time, when he got home from work, Grinch hit the ceiling. He asked Stoney what was going on, and Stoney played dumb. Grinch called the garbage people and raised hell with the dispatcher, who raised hell back. Result—it took two more weeks for Grinch to get another garbage removal company to come to his home and at a premium price. In the meantime, dogs had ripped open the huge pile of bags and crap was scattered all over the neighborhood. Stoney had another friend report Grinch to the police for littering. See the section on *Neighbors,* and if you live near Stoney Dale, be a good, friendly neighbor!

Gates

Always open gates and leave them open when you're dealing with a mark who has a gate. There are lots of fringe benefits to this. For example, his expensive purebred dog might get out and run away. Or, someone or something terrifying could come in. Another benefit of vengeful gatekeeping is that you don't even have to trespass. Just opening the gate is enough.

When I was a kid, we had a mean old man in the neighborhood. He lived on an estate sitting in the middle of ten acres of woods. We used to open his gate all the time, then go on our way down the road. He'd spend an anxious hour or so hunting for us on his land, never finding us, of course. His own paranoid imagination was our best ally. This concept will work well with doors, too. Think about your mark finding open doors or windows in his house.

Genitals

I bet that few other books have a chapter with this title. A reader named Eric P. had an errant young woman do him a nasty once, and he hit back where her ego (alone?) showed.

"I got her worried about vaginal odor. She was vain as hell, insecure about her body, and very sensitive about 'personal things,' including body odors. I started by having a delivery service bring her a present of a gift-wrapped package of liquid douche, scented, of course. A few days later I put together an 'Emergency—Protect the Environment' package containing more products of a personal nature. I had that delivered. I sent a few cards from boys she knew and other friends hinting at this personal problem in broad terms, but never really mentioning vaginal odor, *per se.*

"I then had some memo pads and letterhead printed, using the name The Funky Vaginal Odor Control Board with a fake return address. I started sending these to her and getting friends from other cities to remail them for me. I posted her apartment door with an official-looking statement from the Board, using my letterhead.

"Next, I sent a couple of her boyfriends clothespins with instructions to clip on their noses when dating this girl because of her runaway case of vaginal odor.

"I did a few more things, but I guess you get the idea. In case any reader feels sympathy for the girl, don't. She deserved every single bit of trouble, believe me. I'll never collect what she owes me. But I'm trying to get back a little."

Another splendid addition to the genitals of a mark is spearmint oil. According to several Haydukers, most notably Dr. Schwatzen an Luft, if this elixir is placed on such sensitive areas as the genitals, the mark will really have the hots. The doctor suggests lubricating condoms with this oil or adding it to douching solutions, vibrators, or tampons. It will dry on the surface, then, when activated . . . call the fire department.

Government Mail

Did you ever notice the legend on government envelopes "Penalty for private use $300"? Ah, I bet you're thinking of good ideas already. For example, you could get a good batch of military recruiting material, address it to various individuals who would be sure to inform the feds, enclosing personal and/or insulting notes with the mark's name and address intact, then staple shut. Let's see just how serious those wimpy postal feds are about all this.

According to Jimi the Z, if the USPS is bull-shitting about this legend, then everyone should send his/her personal mail as official government business, using the government's postage-paid envelopes.

"Let's all of us get these government and nonprofit, postage-paid envelopes and mail our personal letters and such in there," Jimi says.

Graffiti

Bob from Everett, Washington, has a twist to the trick of writing your mark's (or his spouse's or sweetie's) name on restroom walls. Bob says to put just the phone number and no name, or use the real number and a made-up name. That last touch will make the spouse suspicious about extracurricular activities.

One of the goals the true graffiti artist strives for is permanency. You inscribe a message, and some diddlesquat civil servant or his lackey comes along and somehow covers or removes it. The Marquis de Amway has discovered a very good way to make graffiti last a lot longer on the job. Here's his idea.

"Let's say that someone has burned you, messed up your car, or otherwise marred your person or property, and you want to graffiti them back, but in such a way that the message will stick. If so, you're tuned to the right guy. Pay attention now.

"Get a piece of paper and spell out 'UP YOURS!' or 'YOUR WIFE SUCKS,' or some other very rude, personal grossity, using Comet or Ajax cleanser to spell the message. Then, spray over the whole thing with Right Guard, English Leather, or any of those sprays that will burn. Test them first. You can also use charcoal lighter or lighter fluid if you want to.

"Go to the home of the person you want to get back at, and tape the message paper to the floor, wall, even onto his car, or wherever you want the message to appear. Next, spray a stream of lighter fluid leading away from the paper, sort of like a fuse. Light that fuse and run like hell.

"WHOOSH, the paper blows up instantly, but there's no fire danger because everything just sort of disintegrates. But the cleanser chemically etches your rotten message onto whatever you stuck it to so well that it will never come off.

"There it is, your message, etched on permanently."

"We've tried it, and this stuff will work on concrete, metal, brick, tile, wood, anywhere. You can 'say' anything to anyone this way, and it will be damn near permanent," the Marquis de Amway tells me.

If it is inconvenient for you to write your graffiti on the spot, you can always use Avery labels, those adhesive-backed units that people use to address envelopes and so on. You can be as gross as you wish, and it takes only a few seconds to stick them into place. They are hard to remove, too.

Gross Music

Here is the Hayduke Hit Parade of rotten music you can use to gross out straight marks, as mentioned in several chapters. Three Zappa tunes come to mind: "Stick It Out," "You're An Asshole," and "Bobby Brown." Use parts of Prince's lyrically offensive selections like "Do Me, Baby." You can also use ethnic, racial, and military music to good advantage, as well as X-rated party records and the very explicit sex-sound recordings now on the market.

Gun Nuts

The worst enemies that gun owners have are their own rednecked mental peewees who write letters to *American Rifleman* and *Gun Week* tying all the gun woes to liberals, communists, and everything else in the world. They are the single-minded adults whose entire lives revolve (no pun intended) around the issue of gun control. Generally, they are from small towns and have IQs to match. If only there were a way to keep these bad examples out of the public media. Oh, well.

Bud Hammell is a gun collector who was harassed by the state police because a fellow collector informed one of their agents that Bud was selling guns to kids, didn't keep sales records, and so on—all untrue. What had Bud really done? He had fairly outbid Mr. Informant on a gun collection for sale. To get back at the jerk, Bud waited a year, then placed some classified ads.

"I put the ads in controversial underground and radical publications—both left and right wing. I advertised "Machine Guns and Silencers for Sale . . . Cheap!"

In his ad, Bud made such clever claims as "I handle all red tape—no forms for you to fill out, no expensive tax stamps . . . no worry with the police or BATF ."

Naturally, the name, address, telephone number, and dealer number of Mr. Informant went on the bottom of the ad as its logo.

Mr. Informant was a licensed gun dealer, but he didn't have the proper license to sell machine guns or silencers. The ads had been out only a week when the first federal agent came to talk with Mr. Informant.

Ask anyone who is a licensed gun dealer or knows the business; it's really bad news to have these gun law feds on your case, especially if you *are* innocent. America's federal gun law cops are the nearest thing to the Gestapo we have.

Ham Radios

Here's more from Millard Plankton, our resident rabble rouser of the radio waves. This time he wants you to get hold of some two meter ham gear. But it new or used, then get a repeater guide from a ham shop and find an autopatch phone repeater in your area. This autopatch repeater will enable you to make free telephone calls twenty-four hours a day, using some fake call sign (an excellent chance to nail a second mark who is a ham operator—use his call sign).

Imagine the fun, Millard says, using a small hand-held walkie-talkie—now with 800 channels on it. He says to call anyone at late hours. It's no cost to you and can't be traced easily because it is radio. But, don't stay on too long; you can be traced directionally.

Hawkers

Dapper Norton O. Worthin is a prissy little wimp, or so he claims. Underneath, he's a true nasty, saying, "I saw your chapter on hawkers and, as an expert in that field, I have some refinements. You can utilize hawkers for mass transit vehicles, or large public crowds in theaters, ball games, concerts, and the like. If you drink a big glass of milk followed by a big glass of pulpy lemonade, you can create cohesive hawkers that are truly works of art."

Sounds like Norton is truly a "fine artiste."

Hayduking

Some of the mail I get is wild. There are some people reading my books who are actually dangerous, badass folks who I would not even want as enemies. Some of their ideas are so evil that even my "literary" competitors wouldn't rip-off these contributions. That's what got me thinking about this idea.

By the way, I'm honored that my name has been turned into both a verb and a noun in the same way that *Watergating* is now a part of the language. Anyhow, two readers came up with the idea of sending the mark a copy of one of my books . . . "and let him think about it for awhile." The trick is to send the copies anonymously. You can also turn down pages, maybe underline some passages in red, or perhaps annotations in the margins would help.

Holidays

Our kindly charities would have you invite every deprived/depraved minority from boat people to orphans to democrats into your home for Christmas, birthdays, and other holidays. Down at the Louisiana School of Living Divinity, the Rev. Tobin Williams has an interesting alternative. He thinks it would be nice to invite some roadkill.

"Imagine the look on the mark's and his family's faces when they're gathered around the holiday tree or festive table as the posthumous guest of honor is unveiled—inside a gaily wrapped package.

"You need an opaque plastic bag, of course, so the mark or his designee will reach in and grab hold of the roadkill. It would also help if this bag is hermetically sealed to hold in the festive aroma until the very last minute.

"It goes without adding that this present must be appropriately gift-wrapped and carded," says Rev. Williams.

Hot Tubs

Carolyn, another L.A. punk rocker, says she once dumped five pounds of fertilizer in a self-styled Lothario's jacuzzi. The resulting odor was quite vulgar throughout the entire apartment complex. Another friend, Mel Cajones, says that someone entering a hot tub or jacuzzi containing this fertilizer broth is quite likely to get nasty skin burns.

I'm not so sure about this one, but as it came in from our very wonderful Heidi Marie, why not try it? After a particularly unhappy party experience involving a hot tub and some very obnoxious people, a friend of Heidi's decided to stiffen up the host's hot tub—symbolically, no doubt. She added several boxes of cream of rice cereal to the tub. It sounds great, something to interest a lot of kids . . . a huge bowl of hot cream of rice cereal.

Household

Do a good deed on behalf of your mark's diet. A bead of superglue around that rubber gasket strip on the household refrigerator door will help that door stay shut and protect the mark from the munchies. See? Not all stunts are totally horrible.

Houses

I'm not sure how practical this is, but you could try to take the rain gutters off your mark's house or apartment. When a huge rain comes along, the runoff will cascade off the roof and probably a lot of it will end up in the basement or house. The rest will turn the mark's lawn into a marsh, as I've seen it done. Be sure to collect some money for your work, though, by selling the mark's gutters to a scrap dealer or builder who won't ask questions.

Or if your mark lives in a brick home, spray paint an obscene word or slogan on the bricks with enamel paint. It has to be professionally removed, according to Maribelle Shoofly.

Hunters

Amazing as it may seem, a lot of people don't like hunters who act like mindless killers or slobs. Let's go for the jerk who happens to be a hunter or whose hunting has caused you enough grief to want to get even. Jimi the Z sneaks his marvelous madness into the field here.

"Once it was imperative that I return some disfavor to a person who hunted. I caused him to receive some custom-loaded shotgun shells. Instead of the usual shot, we loaded the shells with a combination of corrosive salts, coarse sand, tiny lead balls covered with grinding compound, plus steel burrs. We also used flammable padding instead of the normal plastic wadding. You wouldn't believe what a day of shooting those special loads did to the man's shotgun and what *that* did to the man's psyche and budget."

IRS

If you are a printer or have access to a *very* trusted printer, Edwin Sneepf has an idea for you. He thinks it would be a splendid joke to print some fake IRS 1040 or 1040A forms. Make them camera-ready, almost like the originals, but with some very minor alterations in some of the questions. Be creative, e.g., add "shacked up" to the marital status options. Call the taxpayer "dog-breath" somewhere. Use gross language in the small print instructions, insult the infirm, the old, and the minorities. Be crude and rude, then distribute. In addition to Sneepf, this same basic idea came in courtesy of TAP.

Junk Mail

Some of my mail contains questions about how to deal with everyday problems. Here's one that came in often, and I'd like to throw it open to those evil members of the Hayduke Society who love their revenge both sweet 'n' sour.

People want to know what they can do to wipe out junk mail. They are bogged down by torrents of junk mail—all sorts of junk mail—magazine subscriptions, charity fund raisers, buying clubs, porno, religious groups, ad nauseam.

I've suggested a few ideas, but what about the rest of you? Send in your tried and true ideas for dealing with junk mail and junk mailers, and I'll include them in the next book.

Landlords

Their landlord kicked a couple of my readers out, claiming they had violated the lease by holding "loud parties." The landlord's complainant was an eighty-one-year-old neighbor lady who was partially deaf and totally bigoted. Her eyesight was good enough, though, to note that the couple renting was a salt 'n' pepper pair. There had been no loud parties. In fact, there were no parties at all. A quiet couple, their socializing was limited to two or three other couples coming in for bridge once or twice a month. Ho hum.

Not wanting to fight in court, they found another apartment, then decided to fight back their own way. They waited a few months and learned through good intelligence sources that the landlord would be away for a weekend.

They called a caterer and arranged a very posh affair, ordering full service, the best in food, expensive lawn furniture, a strolling band, champagne fountain, silver and crystal . . . the whole bit. All arrangements were handled by telephone. Invitations went out to all sorts of people, including bar derelicts, plenty of minorities, neighbors of the landlord, and, of course, to add to the cover, every present and former tenant they could locate. It was timed for noon Sunday. The landlord was due home by four that afternoon.

Times were tough, and the caterer was only too glad to get the business. Yet can you imagine the business the mark found when he returned home that Sunday afternoon with "his" party in full and very expensive swing? Naturally, all the guests greeted him with thrilled smiles, also asking when he'd open up the house so they could use the bathrooms.

Sputter, sputter, sputter went the landlord. His wife went wonder, wonder, wonder. The caterer went pay, pay, pay. The salt 'n' peppers went ho, ho, ho.

A variation of this same idea was suggested to me by Lynn in Denver. In both her case and the one just mentioned, the vengeance was most fitting, plus being most expensively and emotionally successful.

Not all landlords are as wonderful as you've been reading about. Bob Pursell, who used to live in Boston, told me about an apartment owner who had a "no paint" complex until the kids who were his tenants agreed to paint the place if the landlord bought the paint. The agreement was made.

"The kids painted everything black. I mean everything," Bob related. "They painted the toilets black. They even shut off the water in them, dried out the bowls, and painted the insides of the commodes black. Even the light bulbs were black. The windows were black. If you can think of anything else, they did too, and painted it black. The ceiling was black, the beds were black . . . everything was black . . . except the landlord's face. It was red."

A Chicago journalist told me about his undergraduate days when his landlord refused to fix a septic tank overflow. The smell and the hygiene got worse, and as summer approached, when school ended, the students living in that rental sewer were only too happy to get out.

"We left him a little overflow message of our own about the need to clean up his sewerage. We got back our security deposit and just before leaving, one of the guys, who'd hidden, flushed twenty pounds of powdered detergent down the toilet. We then left, immediately."

Land Rapists

Rooters of the lost ark will appreciate this version of the Piltdown Man. It's a creative way to harass those land rapists who anti-semantically call themselves "developers." You go to the work site when it is dark or otherwise unobserved. You bury some objects like arrow heads, odd pottery shards, human skulls snitched from a bio classroom, and other artifacts. The best way to proceed is to tip off some serious college kids who like to work on digs. Females are usually best for this role as they are more often true believers about this sort of "discovery." Let these kids discover your "artifacts." Hype the find through the local newspaper—especially smaller weeklies. Insist through the local historical society that moral and legal pressure be brought down on the developer to halt his operations until a scientific dig can verify the findings.

Laundromats

Recently, I listened as a young woman related how her roommate would continually come in from drunken orgies, sick to her stomach because of what she had done. On one occasion, she managed to void the contents of her stomach all over the work wardrobe of the young lady telling the story. Apparently, it was not the first time it had happened.

"I pleaded with her to stop getting loaded like that and making it with any guy who asked, usually right in our room while I was there in my bed. I threatened to move out. She was a nice kid, sometimes, but this was the last humiliation and ruination for me and for my clothes. I moved out . . . but that wasn't all. I had to get even.

"A week or so later, when I knew she'd do her laundry, I put my plan into action. After she put her clothes into the dryer and went next door for coffee, I slipped into the laundry room unnoticed and tossed a handful of colorful wax crayons into the dryer with her clothes."

Joseph and his Biblically mentioned coat had nothing on this boozy sex-date.

From our quickie, but itchy, division, if you want to give a person a really uncomfortable day, toss a piece of fiberglass in with wash containing your mark's undergarments. It's guaranteed to ruin his day and, with luck, could also provide a mild rash.

Lawns and Gardens

This is a simple and effective hit'n run tactic to have fun with your mark's lawn. Everytime you walk or drive by the mark's yard, throw a few large stones on the lawn. It all builds up. Vary the size, and you'll not only ruin his mower blade, but you might even get him to sail one or more of these stone missiles through a window or into his car.

I know one friend of the environment who live-traps his Japanese beetles, then at night takes his catch over to his mark's yard and garden and sets the little buggers loose to do their misdeeds there. A refinement of this was suggested by Bob Thornbroug who says to plant Japanese beetle traps in your mark's garden but take the catch bags off the traps.

Scattering weed seeds and other vegetative miscreants into his mark's finely tuned yard is Sid Nerko's way of getting back at manicured lawn freaks.

Lawsuits

According to one lawyer who really does have the Establishment Bar Association stamp of approval, it's fairly easy for you to sue someone. Most states have something called a small claims or citizen's court for just such actions. But you also have individual access to regular state and federal courts, just like those lawyers in the cash-green, six-piece suits. The Hayduke legal adviser says you should go to your local law library and/or courthouse to read some of the books on the topic which legally interests you or in which you wish to sue.

The law library has a set of books containing the exact legal forms necessary to sue someone. Find what you need and have a copy made or purchase a form. Don't be shy about asking lawyers—especially young ones who pop into the room—for advice and help. Don't be afraid to ask a clerk for help, either. Fill in the blanks on the form, asking for help if you need it, and file your suit with the clerk. It will cost you from nothing to about fifty dollars to file a suit.

With that modest investment of your time and money, you can file damages asking for hundreds of thousands of dollars. Think of the stress value and the bad publicity your suit will cause the mark, as you see how surprisingly easy it is to institute a lawsuit.

What if *you* should get sued? Easy. Go to the courthouse and countersue. Most people don't think of that. That's why there are so many losers and so many lawyers out there. Do it yourself.

Lunchboxes

In addition to sabotaging the mark's lunchbox before chow, there is an opportunity for afterwards, too. Clip some disgusting porno pictures, or get a bogus love letter written to the mark, or select some used rubbers or sexy pants, and plant them in his lunchbox *after* he's done with it for that day. The fun begins when his wife opens the box at home that night to clean it out for the next day.

Wouldn't you like to be there to hear the discussion?

Ma Bell

People think that a telephone lock defeats pirate callers. However, according to Toby Bill, telephone locks can be defeated.

"When you dial a number normally, 5 for example, as the dial rolls back to its original position, it breaks the signal the number of times indicated—5 in this case—and so on for each number dialed. That's how a dial operates," Toby explains.

"To achieve the same effect, i.e., 'dialing' and getting a number, all you have to do is tap rapidly on the little button at the top of the telephone—the little part you use to 'hang up' when you put down the receiver.

"Let's say you wanted to call 123-4567. You would tap on that button once, pause half a second, tap rapidly twice, pause, tap three times fast, pause, and so on. It take a little practice to get the numbers right, but it does work. So much for locked telephones," he adds.

If your mark's telephone is the popular "touch tone" type, you can easily render him sans telephone with a few drops of superglue on the buttons. Or as Old Greavy suggested, glue the handset of any telephone to the main body.

If you have access to the mark's telephone, you might want to call in a bomb threat to some company, institution, or government office. The grabber is that you leave his phone off the hook, then you split. The call will be traced, and someone official will come to visit your mark.

Want to reach out and annoy someone? Go to a pay telephone in some very isolated rural area or a dangerous urban area—a telephone few people are likely to use. Call the mark, establish that you are speaking to the mark, then just lay the telephone down and walk away without hanging up. This will render the mark's telephone inoperable until someone either hangs up that pay telephone or the telephone company locates the trouble for the mark.

A lot of banks, post offices, and airports have dialless courtesy telephones with autodialers built in. Their idea is for you to use this as a service telephone or to get help with a programmed number. But, according to another Ma Bell guerrilla, P. Wallington Symms, you can use a standard touch tone phone keyboard—usually available from Radio Shack for about $6.95—to make outgoing calls on these courtesy telephones. Some phone phreaks call these White Boxes. You can get busted for this, so be careful.

When you really want to reach out and touch your mark, call Ma Bell's security people and tell them that it's your civic duty to report that the mark is using one of the dreaded Blue or Red Boxes to make illegal calls. Call either from a pay telephone, or make it more credible and call from some third party telephone. Even better, if you work in the same office or building as your mark, use his office phone . . . or, use the phone of a second mark. But, mainly, let those fingers get busy walking . . . report your phone phreak of a mark for using a Blue or Red Box.

In her continuing war against Ma Bell, a delightful trickster from San Luis Obispo, Ma ReBel, has come up with a secondary mark campaign. As noted earlier, the mention of the dreaded Blue Box causes the Mutha Bell's security people to go into a mouth-frothing tirade of paranoia. Ma ReBel says to have your secondary mark sell Blue Boxes. All you do is place some classified ads in local,or national for that matter, underground newspapers, swinger publications, freak newsletters, protest pamphlets, et cetera. Your mark's ad copy has a big headline which reads "BUY A BLUE BOX CHEAP," followed by an explanation of how the customer can use the Blue Box to make free telephone calls. The ads say nothing about illegality but promise quick, confidential service and that "we maintain no records." You can also use handbills, circulars, and public notices on bulletin boards to advertise. Your mark's name, address, and telephone number constitute the logo for these ads.

If you're the careful sort of person who wears both suspenders and a belt, just in case, you might want to clip one or more of these ads and send them to Mutha Bell . . . from a concerned, law-abiding citizen, of course. Veteran anti-Bell guerrilla fighters tell me this one is 100 percent guaranteed to get Big Mother to come out swinging with all her legal and paraCIA might.

An original Jimi the Z suggestion for the Blue Box is to use yours with your mark's telephone. Use it carelessly and make all sorts of expensive calls so that Ma Bell's KGB agents will come down hard on the mark, thinking he or she is the Blue Boxer. By the way, Jimi says to enjoy your Blue and Red Boxes now, because both will be obsolete within two to four years due to technology. Then, I guess, it will have to be Satellite Box time. Maybe, this is where tapping comes into the picture.

You're in a phone booth late at night. You slip some coins in the slot and call. No answer. You retrieve your coins, dipping your fingers into the narrow slot, hoping for the ridge of a coin.

Slop, warm, gush . . . yuk . . . GUNKY WETNESS on your fingers!

Billy McMillan will laugh, because he was the guy who filled up that pay telephone coin return slot with used, soggy chewing tobacco. The funny part is, you touched it.

Can you think of a good, justified, personal application for this stunt?

What took you so long?

This next trick will work well with any telephone complex but seems to work best on the private operations like PBX, according to telephonic engineer Marvin Basil. If you want to get back at someone or some outfit using their phone system in a rather harmless, prankish way, open the building's telephone wall plate and put a huge magnet inside. The next time one line rings, they all will ring. This will continue until someone either finds and removes the magnet or calls for a service person to do it.

Think of the revenge you can get if your corporate or institutional mark has an INWATS-PBX-OUT telephone system, also known as an 800 line. Get access to such a telephone by visiting an office while its occupant is out to lunch, in conference, on vacation, or away for the weekend. You can pose as anything from an employee to a repairperson. You might want to know the time and weather in Auckland, New Zealand for example. And, you might want to know it often. Call and make some new friends in the USSR, China, or Thailand. Or call Cuba. Call Argentina. If you know the mark's access codes, you can do it in more safety from a pay telephone.

Because of a time lapse between a cost estimate, completion time, and a computer malfunction that was totally the telephone company's fault, telephone service was disrupted for the now defunct law firm of Swinefeldt and Schwanz according to their former office manager, Willi Wegner.

"Our firm's partnership dissolved only partly because of this, but either way, I was out of a job," Wegner claims. "So, in addition to job hunting, I struck out at our mean mother of a phone company.

"I went into a Phonecenter Store, one of those retail outlets where Ma sells her designer phones. I headed for one of her

'Custom Calling' telephones on the wall which are usually white and are sometimes marked 'Courtesy Phone.'

"I called all over the country for about ten minutes. I did the same thing in two other Phonecenters but always altered my calling patterns, even my appearance. Then, I cruised away from there for a good long while," Wegner warns.

I ran this through one of Ma Bell's still-on-the-job employees who is one of us at heart, and he said, "You have no idea how much this irritates management and upsets our security people. Done right, it's fairly foolproof."

Virgil M. Benson has this phony friend named Ray Hastings who cost Virgil a lot of money. It seemed that every party, every visit, every chance, old Ray used Virgil's telephone to call long distance. As the toll charges went up and up, Virgil burned and burned, yet he paid and paid. Then, he read *Getting Even.*

"It was simple, after that. I got a book on telephonic engineering from our library and devised this pay-back method," Virgil writes. "Get access to the B-Box (or whatever your local company calls it) in your mark's apartment complex. It's the little box where all the apartment telephone lines hook up to the main trunk line. It's in the basement or laundry/storage area in most apartments. For houses, they are on the poles.

"Disconnect your mark's phone line and hook up a lineperson's headset—easily available at most Radio Shack stores. Call all your buddies all over the world. Call person to person; call often. Let Ma Bell and the mark fight about who pays for what."

This must be a fairly common scam as I got the same suggestion from six other readers, including one who is a former lineman for Southern Bell. The M.O. in each case was exactly the same. Delightful dialing out there, gang.

It's too bad more people don't know about something known in the trade as "Call Forwarding." In this service, Ma Bell gives you a code which you dial into your telephone. Thereafter, at your signal, all calls to that telephone will be diverted to another number which you dial in after the code. I'd like to rename it "Creative Call Forwarding." Creative comes into this if you have covert access to the mark's telephone and know his codes. If he or she will be away for a few days, why not dial in the proper codes to divert his calls to Moscow, Bangkok, or Perth? According to my friends at Ma Bell, the mark will be billed for all the call diversion services—international as well as national.

Do you know how you can tell when you reach middle age? It's Saturday night, the telephone rings . . . and you pray it's not for you. Ever hear from the Telephone Bore? This is someone who doesn't know when to quit. Or it's someone who talks for twenty minutes and says nothing. Or it's someone you don't want to talk to: a relative, bill collector, salesperson, boss, lover, spouse, employee, or even a Jesus Junkie.

As always, there are ways to handle this unwanted caller. In her magnificent tract titled "Getting Off On the Phone," the famed journalist Tina Rickson lists a number of ways to break off telephone conversations. In the interest of public service, here are some of her better methods.

- "I'm expecting an immediate return call from the White House (or some other Oz-like symbol) and must keep this line open." Hang up and leave your phone off the hook for five days.
- "OhmiGod, there's a police officer running across my front lawn, and he's waving his revolver toward the house."
- "Hold on, the neighbor just came by to say my car rolled out into the street and has traffic tied up."
- "Shhh, listen . . . that strange man who was here a few days ago said he thinks the line is being tapped. Are they after you or me? Hello? Hello?"
- Pretend to be an answering machine by saying, "Hello. I'm not at home right now. But if you leave your name and number, I will . . . "

- Pick up the telephone and scream into it as loudly as you possibly can. The more inhuman the sound, the better.
- Scream an especially scatological or dehumanizingly vile obscenity.
- "Oh oh, my brat overflowed the toilet again . . . gotta go!"
- "Terribly sorry, but I'm taking part in a national poll on what Americans think of registering medflies as illegal aliens, and they asked me to hold this line open for the next two weeks."
- "Do you have any idea at all how awful your breath is? Take a mint or something and call me back in a few years."

Her personal favorite is to record on a blank cassette the sound of a telephone ringing, then switch your tape recorder to the playback mode. When you are faced with an unwanted caller, simply turn on the machine, and that caller hears the other phone ringing in the background. You excuse yourself to answer "the other line."

Sure it's simple. But it works.

Airman Inside has a wonderful idea to deal with the telephones themselves. He writes, "Phones themselves are easily messed up if you have a mark you want to hassle that way. All you do is pull out the modular plug, then paint over the contacts with clear nail polish, let dry, then stick it back in. It's all 'Hello? Hello? Hello?' with no answer."

One more warning: *do not ever trash a pay phone.* There are legitimate emergencies that all of us face, and only an idiot/goon would wreck our only communication with the outerworld. NEVER trash a pay phone! If you ever see or know anyone who has hit a pay phone, Hayduke that mark HARD!

Mail

CP from New York deals with magazine editors who can be very rude about not answering their mail. He turned to a rather gross campaign to get the attention of one particularly rude female editorette. After several polite letters and calls, she had not responded or even acknowledged she was holding one of his articles that he wanted back.

So, he sent her a cute little note all done up on frilly paper and included a little product sample with it. Here's how CP's note read: "Last night I coughed up a lot of phlegm, mucus, and snot into a saucer. This morning I found three cockroaches eating that gooey mess. Somehow that brought you to mind."

CP signed the note, then mailed it and the sample to the editor. No response. But he wasn't finished either.

"At the time I had a friend who believed the most effective way to diet after a great meal was to vomit it back up. So getting a sample was no problem. I packaged that up in a large baggie and sent it off to the editor with a note that said, 'You make me very sick. Need proof? Here it is!"

"Finally, after I sent her a little cage full of two-inch waterbugs and cockroaches, she called me with all sorts of threats about mail harassment. We never did settle my article claims, but I had all the reward I wanted just listening to her rant and rave."

CP calls his next idea the Blank Page technique. It's very simple.

You just send your mark a blank piece of paper. Nothing else. It works on the human tendency to imagine things as being lots worse than they really are. In the event there is a letterhead design you can use with this that would feed the mark's paranoia, then, by all means, use it.

In a modification of that, an old business associate of mine used to send second pages of letters to people he wanted to harass. He'd put in some vague summary of something personally or legally important on that second page, then end with some directive requiring immediate action 'or else.' It was damned frustrating because the mark never knew who sent the letter or why it was really important.

Be aware that using the U.S. Postal Service as your personal messenger for the fist of revenge can backfire. An Illinois man, Steven Jones, was arrested by police after he conducted a mail barrage against his neighbor, Kenneth Gibbons.

"We got about 90 percent of all the magazines ever published," Gibbons told reporters. "We also got pornography, real estate deal offers, record clubs, book clubs, aluminum siding deals, you name it. If it came in the mail, we got it."

The two had feuded over a property easement since 1977, and Mr. Jones spent 1981 getting even by using the mails. Apparently Mr. Jones wasn't too clever and was too open. Police easily cracked the case and indicted Mr. Jones. Pending trial, he was free on $50,000 bond and was facing up to five years in the federal slammer.

As the friendly and fatherly precinct sergeant says each week in *Hill Street Blues*, "Hey, be careful out there." Damn good advice these days as you never know whose side true justice is on.

But sometimes we do. In this case, the weed of direct mail bore bitter fruit. Three Illinois college students were arrested for orchestrating a Nazi motif hate-mail campaign against a Jewish chap who owned a tire shop.

What the young men did was send 100 Western Union mailgrams to Jewish folks in the Chicago area. The Mailgrams carried the following message: "Weiss Tire Company regrets to inform you that we must deny your request for credit after it was determined you are Semitic./signed/Dr. Josef Mengele."

Dr. Mengele was the infamous Nazi doctor who performed ghastly, inhumane medical experiments in WWII concentration camps. In addition to the mailgrams, phony orders for such items as swastikas were placed in the name of Mr. Weiss's company, and bogus ads for used tires at outrageously low prices were placed in area newspapers under the Weiss logo.

Two things are not known about this case: (1) What, if anything, did Mr. Weiss do to deserve this treatment? (2) How and why did the three young men get caught? If the response to the first question is "nothing," then obviously, Mr. Weiss should be reading Hayduke books in his fight for vengeance. I stress again, my books are for victims, to help them fight back against the bullies of any political, racial, religious, sexual, ethnic, or other persuasion.

Mail Boxes

A bunch of ice cubes tossed into a mail box or newspaper delivery tube on a warm day will make the mark's reading very soggy.

Mass Transit

A large bag full of bees, horseflies, moths, or crickets placed open on a seat will do wonders for the morale of passengers on a bus or train. Obviously, at times the most effective schemes are hardly that at all. They are just simple actions. For example, Filthy McNasty says one of the best ways to attack a bus or airliner is to gross people out. The simplest way to do this, according to Filthy, is to vomit in such a way that the other passengers can't escape seeing or hearing your act.

If you feel like being a little more sophisticated, he suggests you let loose sneaky squirts from a CS or CN "tear gas" pen on a bus or train. Another of Filthy McNasty's goodies for mass transit vehicles is to hollow out a light bulb or large Christmas ornament, then fill it with the stinko solution or gas of your choice. Epoxy shut the opening, and place the stink bomb in a paper bag. When you have selected your target area, place the bag on the floor, open the top, then stomp on the bulb. Exit the bus quickly. This one also works well in the office, a gymnasium, party, funeral home, et cetera.

A city bus collided with Jack Bacon's parked car, and the transit authority at first refused to pay him at all, then dragged its feet on his insurance claims. In this case, Jack's no-fault insurance didn't help. Finally getting his money after a year's wait, neo-dirty trickster Jack read *Getting Even* and waited six more months. Then he launched his campaign.

"I had posters printed with the mass transit authority logo on them offering half-fare tokens and free rides for senior citizens during rush hour. I also had printed pads of free ride and half-price coupons, all with official-looking dates and numbers. This scam created chaos for three days and continued the hassle for the authority for three weeks. There were also hundreds of really irritated people and several lawsuits. I was satisfied, though."

Media

CP, our veteran writer and editor hiding out in New York, told me the story of how he got even with an old enemy of his when the man was organizing a convention.

"I prepared what looked like a plausible advertisement for a nonexistent rare book company and paid to have the ad placed in the convention program," CP relates. "My ad was a cutout and paste together jigsaw puzzle. You couldn't tell just by looking at my ad what the picture would be when the puzzle was assembled, of course. I timed it so my ad arrived just at deadline so nobody would have the time or interest to check it out. So it was published just as I designed it."

CP's wonderful puzzle was a totally obscene and grossly disgusting picture that insulted everything his old enemy stood for. The ad also promised that poster-sized reproductions of the puzzle could be purchased from the officer in charge of organizing the convention: his mark.

HBO plus other cable and satellite services are the fastest growing divisions in the television industry now. Engineering rebels and other Power-for-the-People folks have already designed and built Black Boxes for home use. These decode the various scrambled subscriber-paid-for signals like HBO. Ma ReBel suggests having your mark sell these devices. It's just like the trick about Blue Boxes (see *Ma Bell*), only this time the mark will be "marketing" the boxes of the darker color which defraud TV cable and satellite companies. Modify and abuse, I always say.

By the way, it is illegal to sell Black Boxes or even the circuit boards for them. But, as of this printing, it was not illegal to sell or give away the plans for the equipment. If someone sends plans along, I bet George Hayduke will publish them in his next book.

Many of the bluenosed, humorless media savants who said that Hayduking with newspaper ads can get you in big trouble were wrong. At least once anyway. I snorted at their pious ignorance when a South Dakota judge ruled as such late in 1981. An anonymous classified newspaper ad had thanked a named woman for "all those good times you gave me." In this case the mark sued the *Sioux Falls Argus-Leader* for invasion of her privacy. They countered that "good times" was capable of being read in either an innocent or a titillating way and would hardly offend the sensitivities of an ordinary reader. The judge agreed and tossed out the suit.

Medical

Neil Nixon had this nasty neighbor we'll call William F. Smith. Smith's dog was almost as ugly as its owner, especially in temperament. The major difference between the two was that the dog didn't have acne scars. One day the dog attacked and bit Neil Nixon, after crossing two yards to get at our correspondent. The attack was totally unprovoked and obviously unwelcomed. Let's pick up Neil's account (and accounting) of the matter.

"I got some nasty wounds and a fair-sized scar on my leg. I decided to bite back at Smith's ego. I got a medical association letterhead by taking a junk mail piece soliciting research fund support, then making a clean letterhead from it with a Xerox machine. The resultant copy looked just like clean, new letterhead.

"I then used a public typewriter to send him the following letter, slightly revised copies of which I also sent to his wife, employer, and closest business associates, asking for their help in persuading Smith to come out of his sacred closet."

Neil's letter read:

As the leading publisher of medical books dealing with unusual problems, we will offer you $50 if you will allow our photographer to picture your barnaclelike acne condition which is of considerable interest to our readers.

You and your condition were brought to our attention by (name mark's doctor) whose nurse told some of her friends about you. They have described the gross appearance of this advanced stage of acne and suggested we contact you. We are also contacting your close friends and business associates in hopes that they might help convince you to share your sorrow with others, all in the interest of medical science, of course.

Memoranda

Memoranda are part of the interoffice political warfare of everyone who happens to be branded with professional or clerical-level employment. Many memos are written in the tradition of Cover Your Ass (CYA), while a lot of other memos are written because of the insecurity of the writer. Or when some memos are written, they cause insecurity in those who must read them. All this pedagogical pap about memoranda will serve a purpose since memos may be used as weapons.

Let's say your mark has been shafting you during the interoffice status rivalry game. Or he or she has been taking credit for your good ideas and/or blaming you for his or her duds. Depending on the mark's personality, you might want to intercept one of his/her memos before it goes out, hold it a day, then send it back with some horrible message scrawled at the bottom or in the margin. Put some honcho's initials on it. Be careful, though, of handwriting here. Or you may simply want to destroy the outgoing memo, or destroy the response memo, or cause copies of sensitive memos to go to the wrong people. You can easily direct this person's fortune by manipulating his or her memo flow to the wrong people.

Military

As another possibility to earlier suggestions about over-registering for the draft, Col. John M. Himmler passes along his idea of registering legions of phantom people using phony names and addresses. He thinks using Teutonic surnames is great, as is using the names of the fascist butchers currently in charge of the country. Or use the names of foreign dictators, too, as well as our homegrown ones. God knows there are enough to go around . . . and maybe to fight their next war, instead of asking us to do it for them.

Mind and Ego Busters

Select a magazine with a large picture of a face on the cover. With a cigarette or match, burn out just the eyes and the mouth. Mail the magazine to your mark. Do this several times a month at random periods. It is a very eerie experience, according to Dirty Donna, who says she really knows the depths of this psychowarfare. She didn't say she was a witch. But. . . .

Dirty Donna says that she also once sent a sympathy card to her mark's wife. Inside the card she wrote a personal message, "So terribly sorry to hear about your husband's untimely death." She dated the message two weeks in the future and mailed it that day. The date of the death was timed to coincide with the date of their wedding anniversary.

Money

Hedley Herndon from L.A. says that if you can get hold of some counterfeit money you should make sure that your mark gets some, too. This works well if the mark gets drunk and becomes loud, rowdy, and tosses his funny money around like there is no tomorrow. Guess again, folks, there is a tomorrow for your mark—in the federal pen.

Mooning

Shooting moons is a wonderful experience, as many readers have pointed out. Becky Beaver, a famous writer, has done it all over Ohio and Pennsylvania, as her ass is better looking than and as famous as her byline. But there have been a lot of other famous moonshots, according to the mail I get from readers.

Here are some extracts:

- When some prominent mark dies or some other deserving soul gets dead by circumstances which the TV cameras will cover, be sure and moon the funeral ceremony in the semidistant background just when and where the TV cameras are rolling. Maybe the TV editors will miss seeing you. Viewers won't miss it, though.
- Seek out some cult religious organization with a gathering or some uptight graduation ceremony. Moon it.
- Hover around family vacation sites of the type that attract typical American families. Moon them on the freeways, aiming for the backs of their cars, usually out your front window. These moon shots are great because the still fun 'n' innocent all-American kids in the car see your ass before their uptight, pucker-assed American parents do. The kids laugh. Kids are neat. Mooning is neat. Parents usually are not neat. It's hard to imagine that they were ever kids.

Moral Sphincter Muscles

This entry was going to fall into the *Library* category, but the magnitude of stupidity involved caught my attention. As Raul Foldwell points out, the Majestical Majority goes into community libraries and bans books at will. One librarian told our Jimi the Z that she caught some rich, three-piece-suit Jesus Junkies defacing and destroying books their mind-masters told them to waste. Their response when brought to court: "It's God's Will . . . we're doing His work and removing the word of the devil."

Don't fight fire with fire. Only a pyromaniac semanticist does that. Fight rhetorical fire with cold water. Go to your public library or *their* library and deface, ruin, and destroy their books, using the same logic.

Movie Theaters

Saul Nerkmeister was annoyed as hell when he had to sit through a movie with a bunch of teenie punkers who talked, whispered, giggled, smoked, then noisily ate candy from crinkly paper bags. He complained to the ticket kid—a shaved-head clone of the punkers—who just smiled vacuously. Saul came back the following week to take his revenge.

The same gang was at this movie, too. Saul had borrowed a friend's bratty baby, who cried and cried loudly throughout the film. Saul, who had target shooter's ear plugs in his ears, had a jolly old time. He couldn't even hear the punkers cursing him and the baby.

Natural Gas

In previous books, I described hilarious things one can do with natural gas or to natural gas utility companies. Here's how to make your own natural gas odor solution. Ethyl mercaptan gives off an excellent natural gas odor, and it's available from chemical supply houses. One reader used it already, as Ollie Lincoln reports.

"The damn gas company kept me awake all night for three months as they drilled a well in my neighbor's field. He hated it too, but the company held the mineral and gas lease. I got some ethyl mercaptan from a chemical salesman and hit at random around the county over a few nights. I found that an ounce of it placed strategically on or near someone's home or apartment, followed by a warning telephone call, will result in a helluva lot of nasty emergency calls to that gas company in the middle of the night. It was great fun," Lincoln related.

Professor Clothespin of Boulder, Colorado tells of a revenge scam with a natural gas angle. It seems that the Professor had a pal who was seriously duped by an oily, incompetent plumber. The plumber cost this guy several thousand dollars worth of rare Persian carpets one day when a supposedly "repaired" sewer line ruptured due to the plumber's negligence. When the Professor's friend sued this swine, the case was thrown out of court, thanks to some fine print in the plumber's contract.

Here's how the Prof's buddy got even. He arranged for a crazy friend to dress up in a secondhand uniform from the local natural gas company. He even put on a real gas mask he picked up at an army surplus store. Then, at around two in the morning, he went to the mark's house carrying one of those big tool boxes. When the plumber answered the door, the disguised man waved hysterically, shouting orders to evacuate due to a bad leak. "The whole block is gonna blow!" he screamed. The plumber and his family scrammed, of course.

Into the house ran the revenge specialist. He made a hasty tour of each bathroom in the house, filling each commode with quick-setting cement he carried in his tool box. He also threw in some rotten chicken livers and old carp guts. Then he split via the back door.

The Professor reports that the mark was forced to replace every toilet in the house. The fish and chicken innards just added to the fun when the plumber started breaking up the concrete the next morning.

In this case, I'd say the punishment probably stunk more than the crime.

Neighbors

At one time in his varied occupational career, Stoney Dale had a very gossipy neighbor he called Nosey Rosey. She used to sit on the steps outside her apartment to watch which tenants came in at what time, with whom, and in what condition. Stoney says she was a "most unpleasant old gossip who made everyone miserable with her pettiness and nosiness."

Stoney noted what times she sat, and shortly before she went on her salacious sentry duty, he saturated her staircase perch with charcoal lighter fluid. Within seconds the carpeted step where Nosey Rosey always sat appeared to be high and dry. However, when the old battle-ax took her accustomed seat, her body weight caused the fluid to penetrate and soak her posterior and the light summer dress covering it. She didn't feel it until one of the other tenants called the huge stain to her attention when she arose to let him pass. She was mortified, Stoney reports, but it took two more applications to get his point across. After that, Nosey Rosey retired to her own affairs.

Who says our Canadian friends lack a sense of humor, eh? A good fan from British Columbia sent along a newspaper cutting showing how someone Hayduked his neighbor by putting a nasty sign in his yard while the property owner was on holiday. The sign read "New Satanic Church" and went on to explain in detail the doctrine of the "church." On the lawn, the Hayduker had placed a store mannequin in a black shroud and hung a dead chicken on the house. The trickster also put a sign on the front door which read, "Closed Due To Persecution." A large totem was erected with a grinning skull at the top. The entire incident was blown totally out of control by local newspaper and TV media people, much to the chagrin of the property owner who wanted it all forgotten.

Damn smart, our Canadian colleague.

If your enemy neighbor is fleeing to another town and you get his new address, keep up the action. Print a friendly invitation asking one and all of the new neighbors to the mark's new home for an introductory friendship session. You may use as your mark's theme such tie-ins as the KKK, a pro-pederasty coalition, the Communist party, American Nazi Party, et cetera. Send a copy to each neighbor. Also include nearby churches on your mailing list and post notices in neighborhood taverns and markets.

Add another to the long list of what to do when the neighbor's dog messes on you, your family, your sanity, or your property. Wilson R. Drew suggests placement of very fresh dog manure, chicken droppings, or some other odorous substance right next to the intake vent of the mark's running air conditioner. Very few marks check the conditioner, he says, so you get a lasting effect.

A little garbage goes a long way when you're trying to have as many of the other neighbors as possible hate your mark. Herb Bobwander has a beefy way to grease the trap for your mark. When he wants to do a garbage number on the mark, he takes advantage of the fact that most people put out their refuse the night before it's to be picked up.

Herb tells you to smear a lot of hamburger or bacon grease on the mark's garbage can. This will attract every animal—both wild and domestic—for blocks around, resulting in a great deal of noise, fighting, and confusion. All of this will irritate the neighborhood which will blame the mark.

After that scam bores you, take the mark's garbage can down the block and dump it in someone else's yard, or in the bed of someone's pickup truck. Or if there is an open car door, dump it in there. Or, according to Herb, you can dump it in someone's swimming pool. In all cases, someone will find a letter with an address, so your good old mark's in trouble.

As a little refinement, Herb suggests you might want to add some goodies of your own to the mark's personal garbage, e.g., sex toys, bondage magazines, gay letters, fetish things, antireligious materials, et cetera.

They surely know how to be neighborly in Northern Ireland. One such lad, a fine Irish Prossie, actually, passes along this splendid little vignette of neighborliness. It seems his American friend Tom was building his home in a rural area of Oklahoma, near the small town of Goat Testicle. His neighbor-to-be had regressed from the cross-breeding of cretins and Barbary apes. What's worse, he had a teenaged punker son. One morning, Tom looked out the window of his new home and spotted his car up on blocks with all four custom-designed mag wheels gone.

Naturally, Tom found the missing wheels had magically rolled right onto punker son's own car. Neighbor and son were, of course, wired into that incestuous Oklahoma Good Ole Boy circuit . . . you know . . . the ones who think the Jukes and Snopes are high society intellectuals. Tom knew better than to try anything official.

Tom also knew which drinking club the punker son and his father frequented. One evening, he followed them there. Waiting until they entered the establishment and settled in, Tom built a small dam of plastic under the gasoline tank of the pitiful progeny's car, then punched a tiny pinhole in the tank. He placed a glowing cigarette at the crest of the dam and ran to his own car.

"I got a bit less than a mile away when it went up—WHOOOM—most colorful and noisy. Later, I learned that the little peckerhead's car was totally destroyed," Tom said.

He added, "As an afterthought refinement, I think I would

have taken my four tires off first. Oh well . . . . ''

From the epilogue standpoint, Tom says the area Good Ole Boys apparently accepted the revenge as a fortune of war. No one bothered Tom or his property again.

Suppose your hated neighbor/mark leaves his castle for a few days. You can try one of Bob Grain's stunts. He helps out by rolling up newspapers and tossing them around the front door area. He leaves notes on the door to bogus visitors about the owner being away. He cuts the main power off to make the home look more inviting to burglars as this shuts down the alarm system and the clock-controlled automatic lighting. It also has the bonus of cutting off the man's freezer. Hopefully, Bob says, a burglar will see all this and not let your efforts go to waste. Then, as Bob notes, the SOB will get ripped off. Phew!

The Midwest's famed T-Shirt Lady really poured it on when the nasty neighbors messed up her front lawn. These nasty neighbors let their downspout drain its cascades of runoff right through the T-Shirt Lady's front lawn. Not that she was a lawn 'n' grass freak or anything, but she also didn't want a duplicate of the Grand Canyon in her yard, either. After some friendly talk, requests, and other rhetorical devices brought nothing but a continued deepening of Runoff Canyon, she decided that neighborly niceness had all but eroded.

"I waited until the next really heavy downpour. Then, armed with a bit of downspout extension and a couple elbows, I quickly rerouted their drainpipe's firing path from my lawn right into their basement window.''

Notary Seals

Our ideas for buying, stealing, borrowing, or otherwise obtaining a notary seal brought in some ideas on simple, inexpensive ways to create a very passable bogus item. Nasty Ned tells me he simply placed a silver dollar tails up on a stool. Then he placed the document over the coin and stood on the coin/document with a clean, rubber-heeled shoe. Naturally this "notarized" document won't stand close inspection, but how often have you ever seen any American official pay that close attention to "notarized" documents? Nasty Ned has used the tactic many times and says it works for him.

Nuclear Industry

Some members of The Greenpeace Foundation are pretty neat because they ignore the first part of their name and are damn warlike in their aims. Being supportive of those aims, I, too, would torpedo a Japanese or Russian whaler or shoot a seal hunter. But, anyway . . .

In 1982, Greenpeacers plastered 4,000 bogus radioactive warning signs along highways in four western states as a protest against nuclear waste shipments. Many anxious residents and tourists in California, Nevada, Arizona, and Utah called police and other authorities to complain about radioactivity.

Good going, Greenpeace, you have the George Hayduke Sticker of Approval. Nuke the butchering bastards next time!

Nurses

A friend of Mark Lochte recently graduated from USC. As part of his major, he was required to pass a physical examination at the university health center. He had already had a run-in with the crabby nurse there who was more pain than a broken eyeball. He came prepared for the urinalysis part of the checkup by secreting a small can of apple juice in his pocket. Nurse Fuhrer handed him a specimen cup, aimed him at the bathroom, and commanded him to "fill."

"My friend went into the room and poured the cup half full of apple juice. He brought this out to her with a sheepish grin. She snapped at him, 'I said fill it full, bucko. Now get back in there and fill up that cup!' He shrugged, took back the cup and proceeded to drink the apple juice, then headed for the bathroom. The nurse nearly fainted," Mark relates.

Occult

Tiring of Jesus Junkies and other recruiters for the cross fouling his foyer, Barclay Mellon considered the occult as a deterrent. He eventually used other Hayduking measures to rid himself of the praying pestilence but recalled the occult when time came to teach a lesson to a pompous, nosy newcomer who was paying more than a passing fancy to Barclay's young wife.

"We lived in a Bible Belt area where people really took their devils seriously," Barclay told me. "I got a real live occultist from upstate to help me—he was only too glad to get involved. Between us, we had my region believing that the amorous newcomer was also the real live thing . . . a true disciple of the devil. It was easy: a few advertisements in the local weekly, some handbills, the endorsement of the real occultist, and a lot of rumors at local bars."

Offices

This one's more in the field of practical jokery than true nastiness. But as an oldline advocate of that form of fun, I'll vouch for Jerald Jordan's idea for the doors in your office or factory.

"Buy a long nontapered punch at the hardware section of a department store or regular hardware shop. Arrive early at your office and use the punch and a small hammer to remove the pins that hold the two or three hinges to the inner office doors.

"The point is that the doors will open and close a couple times, then fall loudly to the floor. Hide somewhere and watch the action. People panic, scream, faint, have seizures. It's mammoth fun."

Oil Companies

The newspaper sadlines are the same all over the country —independent, small service station operators, which aren't owned by the major oil companies, are being forced out of business. Jumping Jack Flash of Chesterfield, Missouri has his own way of fighting back.

"A large magnet, say from a stereo system, can be placed over the flowmeter disc on a gasoline pump. It will stop the mechanism from measuring how much fuel is flowing into your car, but it does nothing to impede the flow of fuel. Thus, you get your fuel for nothing." Mr. Flash tells us.

At least one irritated reader from California is ready to grease his unfavorite credit card company. His is a credit card problem with a major oil company. He writes that he was a little late with his payment, which he does not dispute, and he paid both the payment and late-charge fee. But the company kept charging him the late fee for several more months. Then they added interest on top of that and wrote nasty notices. He wrote, called, and explained. They added more interest.

"At this point, I figured the hell with them, especially if they wouldn't answer me. Here's how I am doing it. I paid off everything to get a zero balance on my statement. I let it go that way for a month so it would be totally clear.

"I still buy all my gasoline, oil, tires, and whatnot from my local dealer because he's a good guy. But now I pay him in cash. Yet each month, I also charge ten cents worth of something on the company card. The first month it cost them twenty cents to collect ten cents. The next month I charged ten cents more and didn't pay my bill. I let it get overdue. There is no telling how long they'll go on or to how much expense they'll go to collect my overdue dime plus interest. My dealer thinks it's damn funny as he hates the company, too."

Paint

Among your marks, you will find a paint freak, someone who is always touching up his house, car, fence, kids, et cetera with paint. Simply slip some luminescent paint into his bucket or sprayer. Whatever he covers with the concoction will show up eerie as hell at night.

Copper paint is a very effective addition for dressing up electrical circuits. Several readers suggested painting a thin line of copper paint down the insulator of a spark plug, for instance, running from metal to metal. If you do it on only one plug out of four, you can create electrical havoc for a mark's car by disrupting the normal circuit flow. The best part is that 99 out of 100 mechanics will never spot it as the problem . . . and all the while their $$$$ service meter is running.

Parking Tickets

If your mark gets a lot of parking tickets, here's a little extra refinement you might want to use on him or her. Remove the ticket from the car before the mark sees it. Use one of those novelty rubber stamps that features an upraised middle finger to stamp a message on the ticket, then return the mark's ticket to the police. If you don't have such a stamp, then print or type some foul message insulting to police on the ticket. Or draw something on it. Blow your nose on it. Or glue an obscene or other appropriate piece of artwork to the ticket before sending it back. Never include any money, of course.

Parties

Most of us like parties, unless they happen to be right next to where we're trying to sleep, study, read, or whatever. One Baltimore couple put up with people in the next apartment who not only didn't invite them to their blasts, but also made them suffer through the horrendously noisy debacles all evening long, then well into the morning.

"It was all screaming, singing, cursing, and the sound of things breaking and crashing," an anguished Mr. Nice-Guy-Nextdoor told me on a talk show. "The next time it happened we went over that afternoon with some coffee and light food and tried to be nice about the whole thing. They treated us like jerks.

"Their next party followed that same awful script. Only this time I got my tape recorder and very sensitive microphone up against the wall—a typically parchment-thin apartment wall—and recorded about ninety minutes of the hysteria and hoopla. They finally quit about five in the morning. At nine, I put both our huge stereo speakers right smack up against the wall where I knew their bedroom was and turned up the volume on my set as I played back their party to them.

"It took about ten minutes for that anguished couple next door to come over pleading. I smiled and said, 'Hey, I thought you were having such a good time you'd like to enjoy your party all over again.'"

It worked.

Formal and semiformal dinner parties are wonderful settings to create embarrassment if your mark happens to be the host or hostess and you don't mind being the actor in the little melodrama. Phil Anders is an expert at being as rotten as he seems on each page of his wonderful, charming, and witty book, *How to Lose Friends and Influence Enemies* (see *Sources*).

Phil suggests you taste your food, find it repulsive, then spit it out—partially chewed—onto the table. You may also berate the host at this point for serving cheap or spoiled foods. Phil also says to spill food and drink on other guests, then make jokes about it.

If you finish eating before others and are still hungry, Phil suggests you can simply help yourself to food on other people's plates. Other Anderisms for a dinner party include blowing your nose loudly, as often and as messily as possible while at the table, preferably using someone else's napkin, the tablecloth, or your sleeve; belch often and loudly so it sounds as if you're going to throw up; and break wind at the table. "Nothing feels better after pigging out," Phil writes.

Phil Anders is a great guy on your guest list. I wonder if he rents himself out for Hayduking duties. Phil?

If I may add some other similar suggestions, you can also belch or cough while some sweet prig is trying to say grace. Or, you can shot something like "Amen, amen, already, let's get to eating this slop . . . PIG OUT TIME!!!" just as grace is being finished. Be sure to step on the last few lines of grace with your shouts.

Pets

There must be a lot of cruel folks out there, like the delivery truck driver who liked to run over kids' pets (*see Getting Even 2*). I got a lot of "thank you" letters on that one from grateful readers. One reader, Tom J. Mellish, suggested we give an animal hater all sorts of opportunity to have animals.

"Swamp this bastard with animals," Mellish suggests. "Run ads in all kinds of papers, hit those free radio swap shop announcements, try bulletin board notices, advertise anywhere and everywhere. Say something like 'Bring me all your stray and unwanted animals. I'll pay you a minimum of $5 for any animal.'"

Mellish says the second bite is to call the SPCA and local police to report that the mark is getting all these animals for unlicensed medical experiments, occult rituals, pagan rites, and black masses.

Robert Wheaton suggests that you telephone all the local pet cemeteries in your mark's name. Request that a salesman come by to explain their pet burial program. If they don't have salespeople making house calls, get them to at least send out a brochure and give them the mark's telephone number, too. Let them hound him later on, just as his barking Bosco has been dogging your sanity.

Being a shameless lover of animals and a committed friend of same, the death of one of these species upsets me. Turtles are in this special category . . . I like turtles. But when turtles die, they may be used for more than soup. According to naturalist Dr. Crank Johnson, few species smell so terrible as a dead and decaying turtle. He adds, "There are many chemical reasons for this, but empirical observation alone will convince most people. A dead turtle causes a terrible odor."

A dedicated Hayduker needs to ask no more questions concerning that fact.

Laxatives work well on people and superwell on dogs. RLS, from Apple Valley, California uses the old dump 'em trick for getting nontoxic revenge on barking dogs that annoy him. He slips his favorite bowel buster inside some hamburger which he then slips to the canine noise-makers. He says this works especially well with house dogs which cannot control themselves once the laxatives take over their elimination mechanism. This hits the owner hardest, which is good justice.

In nastier cases, where he wants to get some sleep and the neighbor's barking dogs won't lay off, RLS says that a few sprinkles of promazine granules in hamburger will quiet things down. He says it is an effective sleepy-time aid for the dogs, lasting eighteen hours with no ill effect. By the way, that drug is actually a tranquilizer for horses.

This is a switch on the usual "get the dog" theme. It comes from Jimmy Watt, and it relies on psychology. He says, "If you have an obnoxious animal you'd like to murder, don't! Instead, drive the owner mad. Toss some UNpoisoned, plain hamburger in the owner's yard near the dog pen, then call the owner. Disguise your voice or have a friend call. Tell the owner you saw a suspicious-looking person toss something to his dog. Or threaten to poison his dog. If you want to run up his vet bill, tell him you already did so. You can also leave some empty packets of rat poison in his yard at a later date.

Mildred Townsend, normally a mild-mannered public relations person, suggests another solution for an obnoxious dog. "You should 'dognap' the animal, then take it to a boarding kennel for three or four days of expensive care. Ask for the works . . . get all the medical and cosmetic stuff you can order. Give the owner's name, address, and telephone number, then say that 'you' (the owner) will be out of town for three or four days. When the real owner/mark gets the mutt back, he or she also gets a hefty bill."

If a dog or cat is tearing up your lawn or garden, stake out a mousetrap for the animal. Wrap the striker heavily with tape so you don't really blast the beast, but just give it a hard pinch. Bait the traps and set them where the animals have been trashing your place. It always works, according to Gretchen Foowatha.

Pet Shops

The pet departments at places like your K-Mart and other junk emporiums are little more than living hells for pets like lizards, mice, hamsters, birds, and fish. Here's how to wipe out the clerk/mark who works there. Go to the pet department where your mark works and order a couple of goldfish.

He or she will give you a bland smile and offer a baggie full of water and some of those poor sickly fish. Here's what you say.

"Oh heck, don't bother with a bag . . . no thanks . . . I don't want them to take out, I'll just eat them here."

With that, you grasp a fish through the baggie and either eat the whole thing or just bite off its head, depending on how fond you are of fish. Or bite the baggie, and drink it all in—water, fish, and all. Sometimes clerks are really fond of small things, even fish, and they get really upset. If not, most will get sick anyway and may vomit if you're lucky.

Photo Shops

Like bacteria, franchised fast photo service outlets have developed all over the country. Jimi the Z says most of them charge outrageous prices for what passes for speedy, but sporadic service. He wants you to go after these outlets if they mess up your holiday, party, or vacation snapshots.

Before getting down to business, he cautions, "Please don't hassle any of these places unless provoked. Some of the smaller independents and even some chains do really good work and do it cheaply. So make sure you're in the right, then knock 'em over."

Jimi the Z has many scenarios to help you process these photo failures through your own negative exposure to revenge. One of his operations involved obtaining some scuzzo porno pictures and recopying them on 35mm color film.

"I got them processed by a friend, then used the offending photo lab's own envelopes to mail selected photos and negatives to local bluenoses, moral jackoffs, and others of that ilk. I offended many birds with that one pornographic stone."

As an alternative, you might recopy the porno photos, then send them to the offending photo lab for processing in the name of another mark of your choice. Or better yet, put them in the name of the mark's spouse or current love interest. The lab develops the film, processes the order, and the mark gets the picture. Both marks go around at each other over this. This scam costs and costs in material, goodwill, public relations, and emotional stress for all parties concerned . . . except you, hopefully.

If you don't get a vengeful rise out of porno, try something technical instead, says Jimmy. Load some 35mm Kodak Kodalith Ortho film into bulk-loading cassettes (available from Kodak or dealers), then identify it as C-41 color film and deliver it to your photo lab/mark. Processing it will wreck their entire chemical system and cause a lot of expensive down time.

Jimi the Z also suggests you might want to "volunteer" to be the offending film lab's advertising agency. Put ads in the local paper or on radio offering things like "half-price on all processing for this weekend only." Or offer each customer a free roll of color film with every roll they bring in to be processed. Considering that photo labs are always running promotions similar to these, it is easy to place these ads. You can let your anger, conscience, and fortitude be your guide.

Been taking your own porno shots? Let's say your unfavorite lab doesn't like your swinging pictures and do-it-yourself porn. Run ads on behalf of the lab either in the local establishment media or in the underground press. The ads would claim things like, "We develop anything . . . no questions asked . . . we love dirty pix too . . . we buy your good stuff—the raunchier, the better." Sign the ads with the name of the lab or its owner.

Pilots

As a former pilot, I am used to all sorts of stories involving our airborne brethren. I once had another pilot take a dear lady friend of mine along on a trip. He put a bunch of very ungallant moves on her, culminating in a variation of the old "put out or get out" line. Not wanting to join the Mile High Club with him, she declined, and when they landed, she refused to return with this airborne asshole. Instead, she called me and asked me to come get her. Being a good buddy, I did so. I also got revenge for her.

A few weeks later, after the Philandering Pilot had forgotten the incident, I called the FAA Flight Service and filed a Visual Flight Rules (VFR) flight plan for him, using his aircraft numbers. He was on another, unfiled, flight at the time. Then I opened his "bogus" plan. However, an hour later, from an uncontrolled field where security was lax, I called the Flight Service by telephone pretending to be the mark's radio contact and announced that his radios were down and "he" was having a bit of trouble. Then I forgot about it and walked away.

When the FAA effluvia hit the prop wash, the mark—our would-be aircraft Romeo—got his tail chewed, a large bill for a false search and rescue operation, and a warning that one more even minor stunt would cost him his pilot's license. All this had a very calming effect on the man. We probably made him a better person.

Police

The late Hugh Troy mentioned earlier was a king of practical jokers. Once he had a run-in with a New York police officer in a park. The public servant was most unservile, treating Mr. Troy in a surly fashion. The next day, Hugh Troy went to the City of New York Office of Property and Supply and bought a park bench for a good deal of money. He had it delivered to the same park where the officer had accosted him. He and two friends did this before the cop's beat began. As soon as they saw the cop approaching, they picked up the bench and started away with it.

To keep this story short, they told the cop they were simply taking the bench home. They did nothing to resist arrest and didn't show anyone any sales papers, or tell anyone about the purchase until their preliminary hearing. The furious judge asked Hugh Troy why he hadn't told the beat cop about buying the bench. Mr. Troy replied that the officer (a) had never asked him, and (b) told him he didn't want to hear a peep out of him. The judge gave the cop hell right in front of everyone and released Hugh Troy and friends. So much for bench-pressed justice.

Why don't people respect our police? Detroit Jerald tells me this true story of what's been going on for years now in the American automobile industry. It seems when the car companies make a run of police cruisers, word rolls down the line, and many workers break out supplies of food waste, garbage, roadkill, and so on, which they hide in the cruisers at various stages of construction. Supervisors and checkers often look the other way. Car 54, what's happened to you?

Politics

Dr. Neil Barrister, the Hayduke legal adviser, says you should *never* forge your mark's name, seal, or signature to letters advocating violence against public figures—especially a certain chief executive type. Rather, he suggests you send loving letters from your mark suggesting pornographic acts between the mark and the addressee of the letter. This should be a juicy love letter. Tell the politician that he sexually turns on the mark. Make no threats, just nice lovely stuff.

"It works great if this mark is a staunch GOP supporter with no sense of humor. It's even better, too, if you can actually swipe and use some of his business or personal letterhead and envelopes. You can also include these types of letters when you return requests for political contributions," Mr. Barrister notes.

Our resident inside source at the Secret Service tells me that these types of cases are always assigned to very serious investigators with absolutely no sense of humor, personality, or trust of anyone. Perfect.

If you have a typical GOP redneck legislator ruining your home district, you can do what some intelligent young folks did a few years back in one of our upnorth hillbilly areas. One of the youngsters became a mole in GOP circles and after six months got himself on a radio talk show as a guest speaking on behalf of

The Candidate (nee mark). Without going into details, he made
Earl Butz seem like a member of CORE and Mike Wallace sound
like a Chicano . . . all in The Candidate's name.

Porno

Heidi, our wonderful lady from L.A., has a great trick for porno theaters. Load up a small plant sprayer with warm milk or light cream, then at an appropriate part of a hardcore sex film in a porno theater, shoot a blast at some mark's head. The mark will think he's been hit by a load of semen. Maybe he'll go looking for the culprit. Act innocent. Heidi says that being a woman she is never a suspect for this trick. Cum again, Heidi?

Projectiles

A thin-shelled paint grenade can be made using the basics of that old childhood game of pinholing the two ends of an egg, then blowing out the gloop. Use a needle and syringe to fill the empty shell with colorful, permanent drawing ink. Close with glue, locate your mark, then color to distraction. This bit of artistic application comes from Alan Kuenau, another California follower of the Order of St. Hayduke.

Propaganda

A great propaganda story originated with retired Gen. Edward Lansdale, a top pioneer in counterinsurgency expertise for the U.S. military and the CIA. A legend in both the Philippines and in Vietnam, some of his antiterrorist propaganda coups are classics in both countries. His sense of logic and humor, plus his understanding of the cultures and mores of the people are a model that some of our foreign service phonies might do well to study. But enough of that.

Soothsayers are very respected and sought out in the Far East. Knowing this, while on a CIA assignment in the 1950s, Ed Lansdale decided to write an almanac. He filled it with all sorts of prophesies for act-of-God catastrophes for the Communists, terrorists, and others who were on the opposite side of Lansdale's battles.

"Modestly priced—gratis copies would smack too much of propaganda and be suspicious—it could be sold in the Communist North. . . . If it were well done, copies would probably pass from hand-to-hand and be spread all over the Communist-controlled regions," Ed Lansdale wrote later.

His almanac was filled with all sorts of predictions about 1955, written in the people's idiom by a master: Ed Lansdale. It told of very troubled times for Communists and their friends. The almanac went over like wildfire and drove the Communist authorities to extremes to censor it. You know the effect of censorship of anything on people . . . it made them want more.

Lansdale recalls, "To my own amazement, it foretold some things that actually happened. My almanac became a bestseller. It sold out everywhere when it hit the stands."

PA Systems

Almost all large department stores and mall shops have employee and PA phones all over the store. Try to identify the main PA system line button, then locate an isolated station where you can use that phone unobserved. Compose the most objectionable statement you can imagine that you can deliver in about five seconds. Make it gross, sick, insulting, or obscene (best if you can combine all of them). Write it down. Then read it over the store's PA line. Hang up the phone and walk briskly away. Look as shocked as the rest of the customers in the store who heard your message. Do it again another day or at random intervals. Always end by saying, "This message brought to you by the management of (*store name*)."

Public Utilities

When Joe Copcheck gets wound up, it's tough to stop him. This time he wants to settle the score with the utility companies and their hands-in-pocket government agency friends who help to screw us all. Joe says, "I saw some legit ads for something called an 'Energy Awareness Seminar' sponsored by our local natural gas company. I thought it would be splendid to place ads for bogus seminars for your company or institutional mark.

"The kicker would be to offer free weatherstripping, free cookbooks, flue dampers, and stuff like that for everyone who attends. Make the seminar for evening hours when it's likely offices will be closed and no officials will be there. Boy, will people be upset because even if the mark gets on the media and denies the seminar, the word will never reach everyone."

Joe twisted his energy conservation screw a little tighter with a recycled version of the recycling drive. Joe says, "In my version, ads and public service announcements would have all the scrap and junk delivered to the business office of your least favorite utility or appropriate government agency.

"Check current prices for scrap, then offer to pay a bit more. Perhaps you could combine all or some of my ideas at once. It might just cripple the bastards for a little while. At least, they'd know we are out here hating their profit-gouging guts."

For this next number, you'll have to assume the name of some official-sounding person, get a telephone drop number, and someone to answer that telephone for a few days. You will be going around to talk shows of various radio stations to arrange interviews as a "consumer relations official" of whatever public utility you wish to harass. It's not hard to do this; talk shows eat up guests and are always looking for more. Sound interested, sincere, and informed . . . a perfect radio guest. Then when you get on the air, sound very reasoned and nice, but let your message be pure fascist or socialist, whichever will upset the maximum number of listeners.

One reader, Ron Fattman, did this number on a southwestern water company recently when he went on to talk about mandatory water conservation plans. Here are some "official" company policies he announced on a major station talk show:

- An immediate ban on all aquariums and noncactus ornamental plants both inside and outside all public and private places.
- All human and pet corpses are to be completely dehydrated in company factories to remove all usuable water before burial or cremation.
- In one month's time, fresh water will be shut off to private homes two days a week and to industry three days a week.
- Citizens will be urged to buy filters to purify dishwater and bathwater to be recycled for drinking purposes.
- Mandatory metering on the number of times toilets may be flushed.

Puzzles

Do crossword and other puzzle freaks bother you? Why is it that they always ask the most disinterested person to help in solving their damn nuisances? Why don't they bother each other? Helpful Harriet offers some advice for dealing with these puzzle addicts. She would pretend to study all the cross clues, make a point of "hmmming" and "ooohhing" a bit, then would fill in a bunch of close-but-wrong answers, in ink, of course. She always apologized minutes later when the puzzler realized the contest was then unworkable. But soon these addicts recognized her for what she was and didn't bother her anymore. Sounds good to me. But then, anyone who does a puzzle in ink deserves whatever happens.

Record Departments

Like many other businesses and services, the recording industry has their circular version of cutting corners. According to an article in *Rolling Stone,* more than 30 percent of the records released today are below acceptable standards in some phase of manufacturing. The reporter estimated that nearly 20 percent of the tapes are ripoffs, too. Add to those musical mistakes the fact that many large retail outlets could care less about the quality of the product for which they take your money.

Our ubiquitous Jimi the Z has a response to this record madness. If a store hassles or cheats you, Jimi says to go in and erase their tapes. He cautions that true record shops rarely cheat or hassle you, so unless they deserve trouble, leave them alone. For the others who cheat the public with commercial slop, Jimi the Z uses an E-bow with an off/on switch installed.

"You can also buy or borrow a small portable eraser from your local electronics store. Whichever you use, wave it fast over the tape display repeatedly. It works," says this veteran erase artist.

Religion

Aron Kay is a dedicated old Yipster who probably still hates everything established and controlled by the ruling junta of the U.S. Thus, Aron Kay doesn't trust religion's newest cottage industry: the Born Again Convert/Recruiter. He calls them the McDonald's of religion. I call them Jesus Junkies. Either way, they are trying to inflict their own lifestyle on the rest of us. Theirs is not a live-and-let-live world. It's a slave/master relationship. I don't want to be anyone's slave.

Aron Kay wants to disrupt established religious services. He doesn't like any religion.

Perhaps that's why we have freedom of religion—so we might also have freedom *from* religion. Here are some of his methods for turning your other cheek in Haydukian defiance.

- Wear clerical robes to a service, remove them, then streak the group . . . buck-assed naked.
- Smoke a joint during services or when they're in your home. Offer the Jesus Junkies a hit.
- Plant marijuana in their church yard or in the floral altar.
- Pie the religious leader.
- If the group holds orthodox views regarding pork, walk into their midst leading a pig on a leash.
- Wear a devil's costume and mask to meetings or when they come to visit you.

Mail still pours in for me all the time asking, "What can I do about the religious cuckoos who come to my door all the time?"

Thanks to Corkie Puckle, we have another answer. He has a method for dealing with door-to-door religious nuts who are total mental fruitcakes.

"Most of them show up in the early evening or on Sunday morning," Puckle says. "I'm a skinny runt, so I just show up naked at the door. Most of them are assertive,and the women are dry, professional virgins in their unused forties.

"They start to hand me a pamphlet, and then they see I am naked. I smile, reach out to them, and say, 'Hi, I'm Corkie, and I'd like to screw you and eat your Bibles. But it's OK if you don't have a Bible. . . . ' "

Corkie adds, "As soon as I tell them that, I offer them a slug from the quart of beer I have in my hand, then ask them if they want a chaser, too."

And readers think I'm nutty!

If a religious recruiter is bothering you and just won't take your usual verbal "no" or a slamming of your door for a negative response, try this number. Write a really spooky "parchment 'n' blood" bill of sale stating that the mark, by full name, has sold his/her soul to the Prince of Darkness, to roast eternally in the fires of hell in exchange for some worldly possession the mark may have won or purchased recently. Send it to him by registered mail, and also send a copy to his religious mentor.

"Let's say the mark has won a lottery, a bingo prize, a church raffle, something, anything," claims Raoul Swansong, a former Moonie. "It can be anything as long as it's material and worldly. This works best with the true fire 'n' brimstone types or the serene, high-on-Christ types. It will keep them away from you."

Another reader sent me a newspaper clipping about a religious fanatic who literally burned a small inheritance of a thousand dollars because he had received a "mysterious letter from Hell telling him the money was in exchange for his soul." He was sent away for psychiatric observation when he told police the devil had tricked him. I wonder what Flip Wilson would think of that?

At least one tribe of organized Jesus Junkies made Oliver Norton's life miserable by converting his mother and her money to their dubious cause. Ollie decided it would be better to join than to fight. Here, in his very own words, is what he did:

"I got a Goodwill suit for a few bucks, washed it in my sewerage overflow, rubbed garlic and cod liver oil into my shirt, swore off toothpaste and mouthwash for three days, and stayed on a strict diet of loads of onions, kippers, hardboiled eggs, cabbage, green chile, and beans. I put a lot of Vaseline in my hair, then went calling on upperclass neighborhoods as a representative of that particular church. I also went into malls and businesses. I went to meetings of the local council of churches, representing 'my' church, after I'd called the real representative and told him that the meeting was postponed."

You can imagine the fire 'n' brimstone fallout caused by Ollie's infiltration. He kept this up for ten days, then went on a preplanned, three-week vacation, returning home fifteen pounds heavier, four shades more darkly tanned, and with a beard.

Restaurants

One of the biggest restaurant complaints I get on talk shows is about soured, spoiled, bad-tasting foods served at the family-type, sitdown places. David Muridae of Chicago employs our animal friends for getting even here.

"Animals are my principle means of gaining revenge on restaurants which serve me poorly. In most people's minds, mice and restaurants don't go well together," David writes. "You take a small container of mice into your mark-restaurant. When you've paid your bill and are ready to leave your table, invert your water-glass either on the floor by your table or on the table top itself. Of course, before you invert the glass, it is important that you have placed a mouse in it. Actually, you may do this to several glasses if you wish.

"As it is dark in many restaurants, the waitress will not notice the mice under the glasses at first. When she does, she may scream, attracting attention. Or she may knock over the glass accidentally while clearing the table.Or perhaps new customers will get there before the table is cleared, and they will discover the mice."

David has ideas for buffet, cafeteria, or salad bar operations, too. He suggests you arm yourself with several dead mice or a small rat before you venture to your culinary mark's establishment. He continues, "Palm one of the dead animals as

Although this will work for many businesses, it came in as a restaurant trick. Stoney Dale of Lexington, Kentucky was fired from his job as a waiter because he turned down the boss' sexual advances. Since turnover there was high anyway, Stoney waited only two months to get back . . . in the hottest part of summer.

"I went to a local poultry farm and got six hens that had recently expired. That night I tossed them on the flat overhead passway leading from the street to the nympho's restaurant. Needless to say, in about two days the place developed a very fowl odor, and a lot of customers complained. It took the boss and some other ninnies a week to find the maggot-infested remains, remove them, and try to clean off the odor. But it persisted for weeks."

A traveling salesman related how a friend of his met him for breakfast one morning at a motel restaurant and was prepared to deal them some misery . . . having been insulted, overcharged, underfed, and kept awake during his previous stay there. Out of a paper sack, he withdrew what looked like a pitcher of pancake syrup, just like the pitcher used at this restaurant. His pitcher went on the table, and their pitcher went into the sack. Only his pitcher contained motor oil.

Napoleon is a reader-turned-contributor. His father is a restaurant chain maintenance man who says the rottenest trick a customer did to get back at the owner was to order a meal that included mash potatoes. He left the potatoes on the plate with ball bearings buried in the food refuse. The kitchen helper hosed you go through the line. Then using the edge of your own plate to cover the action, drop the body on a dish or bowl of jello. The trick is to do this as quickly and naturally as possible."

As a postscript, you can also leave a customer relations message amid the little patio tomatoes, under lettuce leaves, and, of course, in one or more of the dips. Can you just imagine stuffy Aunt Abigail spooning up her favorite house dressing only to discover a soggy rodent corpse? Speaking of broadcasting!

the food and bearings off the plate and down into the garbage disposal. Few disposals can handle ball bearings; it takes a repairperson to undo this trick.

No nice, All-American kid comes cleaner than Roger Justick. That's why I wondered what happened when he was asked to leave a restaurant. It seems he was being too nice, and that made the manager suspicious. While Roger worried about it, some of his friends did something about it—from the inside. Here's the story of a deep-cover agent; let's call him Randy.

"I was hired to bus tables and I did it for a day or so to set things up. The place had those big metal cream pitchers on the tables. I used to drop a huge lunger (see *Hawker*) in each one of them for two mornings, before deciding to go on permanent vacation back to Florida. What did I care about the restaurant owner-mark? He screwed my friend, Roger."

Return Envelopes

Always salvage business reply envelopes you receive in the mail from institutions, businesses, government agencies, et cetera. Especially good are envelopes that were not sealed well or that you opened without tearing. Or if you can get a supply when you are visiting an office, keep that in mind, too. These make great containers for sending materials to your mark, as they identify a second mark for the first mark to puzzle over as he or she ponders "why me" in reference to the contents of your parcel.

Return Postage Guaranteed

The next time your magazine sheds a blizzard of business reply cards in your lap as you read it, think about returning them to their rightful owners. Recruit Blue of the USAF has a fine response.

"Send 'em all a penny, taped carefully to the card. Use the horrible filament tape that nobody can remove. They pay the postage on this, so it will cost them money to recover that penny, and the law says they have to claim it if you filled out the card, made a contribution, and mailed it in."

Rock Stars

Want to create a riot in your town? Want to make the life of a record, music, or video store manager miserable? Advertise that a cult rock or film star will make a nonscheduled appearance at the mark's store. You have no idea what sort of damage will be caused by a few hundred hardcore fans when their idol doesn't show up and the ugly word "hoax" goes through the crowd. Maybe you could be there to spread the word.

Roofs

Windy City Pat told me about a roofing company that contracted to do his home and not only overcharged him, but didn't do their job properly either. It took all sorts of threats to get them to make things right. It took so much grief and hassle out of Pat that he decided to do something about it.

Pat recalls, "I talked with a friend of mine who was a city building inspector, and he told me an old roofer's dirty trick. Toss a couple bars of plain soap into the tar bath used by the roofing company (Pat's mark). I did this unobserved during a lunch break, hitting all three baths they had going on a large industrial project. It made the tar bubble over in all the wrong places, took them three days to clean up their mess, and some money to settle some potential lawsuits for the spillage."

Rotten Egg Smells

When I first heard this one, it brought back memories of mass menu recipes I ran into when I was Uncle Sam's guest. You know, 195 gallons of this, eighty-six pounds of that, sixty-one carcasses of these, several bales of whatizit, and so on. Anyway, this is a recipe for making a massive quantity of a solution that, according to its chief cook, smells *worse* than terminally rotten eggs.

The Rev. J. Richard Young is our mass-amount chef, and here's his recipe: Boil twenty-five pounds of sulfur in a fifty-five gallon drum over a hot fire, adding fifty pounds of lime and water. After hard boiling for an hour, kill the fire and let the mixture sit overnight to cool. Carefully siphon off the yellowish/orange liquid, but leave the settled lime and sulphur. Fill the drum with water, stir the mixture, and bring it to a boil again. Let it settle and cool for another night, and again pour off the liquid.

According to the good reverend, you should now have about thirty to forty gallons of stock. To this, add one pound of sulphate of ammonia fertilizer for each gallon of liquid you have. Stir it, and then cover the mixture. After an hour or so, it will stink awesomely, and you are advised to cover it tightly. To quote one witness who attended its use once in Winslow, Arizona, the afflicted area smelled "worse than if every sewer in town had backed up fully in the middle of summer . . . It was sickenly gross."

Snowmen

You remember back in your days of innocence when you'd see little kids building snowmen during our old-fashioned and benign winters? The tykes would work all afternoon perfecting their masterpiece. That evening, lowlife older kids would come by and kick it and tackle it, bashing it down. Or older derelicts would drive their cars into the little kids' snowmen, destroying everything.

Consider, though, what would happen if these little kids got some advice and help so that they built their snowperson around a fire hydrant, a cement pole, a tree stump, or something else that would give a person or a car equal or worse impact damage.

Sources

Following are sources of information, equipment, supplies, and other goodies that a Hayduker needs. This list supplements earlier source listings in my other books.

Anders, Phil. *How to Lose Friends and Influence Enemies.*
    Dallas: PZA, Box 12852, Dallas, TX 75225
—This book is full of wonderful arrogance and ideas. Try it, you'll hate it, and that's good.

Beat the Heat. Ramparts Press, 1972. Available from RECON,
    Box 14602, Philadelphia, PA 19134
—A good what-to-do-if-busted guidebook.

Capitol Fireworks
1805 W. Monroe Street
Springfield, IL 62704
—A good source of various fireworks displays, units, and components, they sell a catalog for $2.

Center for Study of Responsive Law
P.O. Box 19376
Washington, DC 20036

—This outfit is a resource center for law abuse by major corporations, government, and others who pick on little people. Their best feature is the books and pamphlets they have for sale. Write for their list.

Cohn, Roy. *How to Stand Up for Your Rights and Win.* NY: Simon & Schuster, 1981.
—An excellent how-to book by the most pugnacious and expensive trial lawyer a vengeance seeker could ever hope to have. His book costs a lot less then he does and is full of excellent advice. You should have this one in your library.

Douglas, Jack. *Benedict Arnold Slept Here.* NY: Pocket Books, 1975.
—A funny book by a very witty writer, this particular tome has some excellent paybacks, stunts, and very dirty tricks from about page 124 through to the end of the book.

TAP is an informal newsletter that tells you everything you need to know about dealing with electronic ripoffs and technovengeance in the public utility field. It is totally a reader co-op operation. Technology of the articles runs from very basic to complex. You will find unique information on lockpicking, vending machines, how some people are hooking up free cable TV, how the fake birth certificate ID scheme is run, phone phreaking, TWX phreaking, computer phreaking, free postage, free Xerox, free electricity, free gas, and more. Write TAP, Room 603, 147 W. 42nd St., New York, NY 10036

WESTECH CORP.
P.O. Box 593
Logan, Utah 84321
(801) 563-6401
—An excellent source of materials for building fireworks and pyrotechnics. They have an excellent catalog for just $3.

Sperm Banks

This slippery little trick ought to get up the dander of most people. So we owe a special thank you to a good friend, Dr. Wilbur Nosegay. To start this one, you need to make some Xerox machine letterhead that says something like: "Reproduction Researchers" or "Sperm Donors Anonymous."

The operation begins when you use this letterhead to prepare a solicitation letter to your mark, enclosing a vial or tube with the letter. Tell the mark you are paying ten dollars for a shot of his sperm. Enclose a medical form for him to fill out noting name, age, date, IQ, race, and time of emission. This one is perfect for multi-mark use, too.

If, God forbid, any mark is stupid enough to comply and you should somehow get the vials returned to a real post office box (this is all in theory, of course), you can simply remail them to the mark's girlfriend, wife, mother, minister, et cetera. In reality, it is best not to use your real post office box on your return address. If you're smart, that box number will belong to some secondary mark.

Supermarkets

Filthy McNasty is a true suburban guerrilla. He tells me that you can harass a supermarket by planting smokebombs—which always excite shoppers, especially if you and some cohorts fan the fear by panicking and screaming "FIRE! FIRE!"

He also suggests you can trap and let loose wild critters in a market. Opossums, rabbits, mice, lab rats, and squirrels are all good guests to introduce to the market. Birds do well when released into a crowded market—both small, dirty nuisance birds like grackles and the larger ones like pigeons.

Add a few dead roaches to a large bag of crickets, which you can get from a bait shop, and let this loose in the market. Most people will assume the crickets are really cockroaches. This is great for cranking up the rumor mill, too. Filthy says if you can display some roadkill or dead lab rats in with the real goodies for sale in the meat cases, it will help things along.

Don't go shopping with S 'n' M from Ansonia, Connecticut either. He gets back at nasty supermarkets by using a strong pin and sticking holes in the bottoms of milk cartons and plastic soda bottles.

"With a little reconnaissance, you can also discover where you can either turn down or shut off freezers and coolers in the store. Also find a new product called 'Magic Shell.' It is intended to form a sweet shell over ice cream. Happily, it makes a hard shell on anything cold," S 'n' M says.

"It is especially hard to remove if it hardens on glass. How about putting some Magic Shell on your mark's car windshield or on his home picture windows? If you leave it on half an hour, it's a bitch to get off, and overnight, it is almost impossible to remove."

"Once a really stupid mark thought he'd try to be smart, and he turned on his defroster to melt the Magic Shell off his windshield. All the melted goop ran down into his engine through the air vent on the hood, screwing him even more. I loved it."

Sweepstakes

The reason that con artists succeed is that people are basically greedy and sometimes a bit dishonest, e.g., most folks want something for nothing, and all of us are bargain hunters. That's what Casey Rolands of Tampa, Florida had in mind when he shared this scam.

"All you do is call thirty or forty people in your city and read a written statement which you present after making them identify themselves. You tell each person something along the line of 'Congratulations, (name of person called), you've won our free telephone (name some other secondary mark like a business or radio station) sweepstakes. No, this is no gimmick and not a sale. It's just our free sweepstakes to show people in (town name) how much we love 'em. To collect your prize call (then give them the mark's number) and ask for (mark's first name).' "

You may answer questions but always seem excited and urge them to call today, as Casey adds with a laugh.

"If you want to build it up a bit, identify yourself as being from some local outfit that regularly gives away huge sums of money. It works so well that irate people will call the mark for weeks wondering what happened to their prize money," he says.

Sweethearts

Here's an unusual case of a wife striking back at a straying husband. This clever ruse starts with the wife sending a brief note to her husband's lover, setting up a clandestine, surprise dinner rendezvous for two. The note says it is all a big surprise and not to call or ask him about it . . . big secret stuff. The note hints at good things like divorce, carrying the lover away, remarriage, et cetera.

The next step is, of course, not to let hubby know about this dinner date. Wait for about fifteen minutes after the appointed hour he is supposed to meet lover and call the restaurant. Page him. Lover will probably answer. Wife then says to the other woman, "Would you please ask my husband to come to the phone?" The rest of the conversation should be played by ear. The main idea is that the lover will wonder, how did she (wife) know????

Revengeful Rebecca Between the Slices of Rye (honest, that's the way she gave me her name) says she learned that her old man was playing around, so she started leaving those sexy-style men's underwear in her car, after putting thick stains and baby oil marks on them. She also started leaving a different brand of cigarettes around the house and once put a cigar butt in the unflushed toilet. She alternated between being very passionate and very played out in bed. She made his ego miserable.

I talked to Jim Flasherman just before leaving Chicago's blizzard-swept O'Hare Airfield one summer day. He's really a radio personality, and he passed along a great idea for releasing some stress and emotional pain in the direction of a former lover or wife who is sharing her body, affections, and/or loyalty with someone else.

Jim says, "This works best if your ex is on welfare. You simply call the welfare office as a good citizen and turn her in on prossie (prostitute) charges. Or you get a friend to pose as a cop and do the same. As gilding, get a bunch of other people to make the same complaint. You have no idea how much trouble that causes."

I checked this with a law enforcement official in another state, and he told me that most agencies surely would check it, even if the woman were not on welfare. Significantly, though, he told me, "Women alone, especially divorced women, are very vulnerable to this sort of thing. You know how society and the old double standard are. It's nasty, but it's effective."

Tailgaters

When moldy motorheads used to drive up behind me in the typical tailgate approach, I used to slow down to fifteen MPH. But this usually inconvenienced me more than it irritated them. I was overjoyed a few years ago when I saw a bumper sticker on a car parked in a small lot near Washington. It read *Honk if You're an Asshole.*

"Perfect idea," I said aloud to myself. "All we need to do is add the word 'tailgating' before 'asshole' or 'tailgater' after it."

Another antitailgating tactic comes form Wise King Cobra who uses a two-phase toggle switch to back the bastards away from his vehicle. His first switch is hooked to his brake lights, and when some yo-yo crawls up Cobra's bumper, he hits that switch. A few flicks and some tailgaters back off. Others need more of an adrenalin boost. That's what the second switch is for. It is hooked to the Cobra's backup lights.

"It's damn tough to follow someone as close as tailgater does and not get that loose-bowel feeling when you see backup lights flare up right in front of your face. They *always* fall back after that. I've even seen some run off the road. That's a wonderful feeling."

Teachers

Poor school teachers really do get dumped on a lot. It's too bad because there are a lot of nice teachers. So please don't pick on them just because they happen to be your teachers. Remember, a lot of them aren't much happier about all this than you are, and sometimes they're a lot nicer and more civilized than you are.

Of course, there is always the exception who must be dealt with. On one talk show in New Orleans, a caller named Dan told me about his shop teacher accusing kids of stealing tools from the supply room. The kid he really jumped on for theft was totally innocent and said so—finally, very loudly. He got sent to the office, and draconian discipline came down upon him.

"We decided to get even," Dan relates. "That teacher knew who really took the stuff, but he's afraid of this big kid, so he blamed a little kid and covered it up that way. We figured if this teacher was such hot stuff and was so concerned about 'hot' tools, we'd fix him right up. Just before he was to give us a demonstration on using pliers properly, we heated the handles of his pliers with a torch. Isn't there something in the Bible about burned fingers and thieves? Anyway, it was a just dessert."

The Bible, Dan? Really!

Telegrams

Claude Pederast, a former Western Union employee, writes to inform us that his ex-employer has an unofficial habit o reading customer messages in a covert fashion.

"Western Union computers are programmed to hit on certain key words when they automatically process telegrams," Claude informs us. "Words such as *gun, drugs, sex, assassination, terrorist, riot, and conspiracy,* will all trip in the computer."

I'm sure our readers could make good use of this intelligence.

As you already know, the late H. Allen Smith is one of my favorite humorists. He used a worthy technique on a mark, sending him an express telegram that read, "Vital that you ignore my previous telegram." That's it. That's enough.

Telephone Answering Machines

As always, Jimi the Z has an answer for these mechanical monsters. A gentle starter from Jimi is for you to record the mark's own opening lines, then when his machine beeps for your message, play back his own lines to him. With luck, the mark will think his machine is screwing up and take it in for costly unnecessary repairs. Do this a lot; it works well.

If your mark is likely to react badly to scary things, try this approach. Tape the voices of demons telling the mark evil things. Use your creative imagination for background and voice style. Use messages that create paranoia and stress, such as his/her mate having sexual relations with animals, necrophilia, et cetera. Quote the darker passages from Milton, Hitler, Poe, Goethe, Mick Jagger, Ron Reagan, or Phil Anders. Study the instructive parts from *The Exorcist* for help there.

Terrorism

A great scam for these tumultuous times is to turn your mark into a terrorist. Ginger from Tampa was bothered by local rowdies and hoodlums who terrorized her and her elderly brother. Her son suggested that since the neighborhood hooligans were acting like terrorists, they might as well get full recognition. He went to a hardware store and bought pieces of plumbing pipe and end caps.

"I stuffed some of the pipes with sand, drilled a small hole in the middle, and stuck in a 'fuse,' actually a piece of cord covered with glue. I put the end caps on. Then I put a few more of these 'bomb components,' including an empty black powder can in a paper bag," the son wrote.

"I planted this bag under the seat of one of the hoodlum's cars, then called police and reported terrorists driving that car and waving submachine guns around. Within an hour, the car was spotted, the young owner was rousted, his car was searched, and the fun was on. I also called local TV stations to tip them off, and one reporter actually showed up with a camera and shot film to use on the air. The parents were furious with their kid and didn't believe his plea of innocence anymore than the police did. It slowed the hoodlums down a lot because the police kept watching them after that."

We live during insane times, and a good trickster will take full advantage of this fact.

TV Sets

This one is not a do-it-yourself project unless you have some solid electronic knowledge. It's from Dweezle Moonunit of L.A. and he says you should know that building illegal transmitters is a violation of federal law. But lots of other things are too, including bribes, payoffs, campaign contributions, et cetera.

Dweezle says that for about twenty-five dollars, it is possible to build a small transmitter that will screw up your mark's TV reception far better than any garden variety CB or unfiltered ham set.

"This small, battery-powered device should be operated near the mark's antenna, cable connection, or TV set itself. You will have to design it for the distance factor from the mark. Use Ni-Cad batteries so it will operate for weeks," Dweezle writes.

"Who would ever think a clandestine transmitter is interfering with TV reception? Nobody would. Your mark will spend uncomfortable hours and scarce dollars with repairmen. You might even hope for the mark to blame his neighbors, which would create secondary fun for you."

Not having his green card, but owning lots of greenbacks from his illegal job as a member of The Committee to Re-elect the President, Argentine-born Jesus Hitler bought a color TV set from a large discount store in West L.A. The set was a true lemon, and he wanted his money back. Jesus tried all the traditional consumer stuff that Ralph Nader tries to teach. The store stonewalled in his face.

"I got several small magnets and placed them on the screens of many of the TV sets on display in the store," Hitler reports. "I was told that the magnets would attract particles from the electron guns of the TV receiver to that one spot and burn a 'hole' in the tube."

It worked well, reported Jesus.

Another attack on the TV set is to take a large handheld tape eraser and run it over the back of the color tube—the "neck" or part that sticks out in a hump. This will mess up the color alignment and could injure the line scan, too, if you're lucky.

Typewriters

Do you know a typist who wastes her time and the company's doing personal letters or typing term papers for outside money on company time? Do you know a typist you just don't like for some reason? If that typist has one of the various typewriters that uses a ball, cover the ball heavily with either clear nail polish or a clear spray paint. It gives new meaning to the concept of invisible ink.

Urine

As many readers have pointed out, urine is a wonderful weapon in our arsenal. But did you know three-week-old urine is the ultimate weapon?

While attending a rather wild party when he was a young Marine, Old Sarge got blotto and passed out. His "buddy" urinated all over his sleeping friend. Told of the event by other troopers, Old Sarge allowed some time to pass before getting even.

"I peed in a butt can (a No. 10 juice can) each day, then poured that into some plastic gallon jugs. We had a storage area in our barracks, so it was no problem hiding it. My 'ole buddy' was a lance corporal and had his own room in the barracks. Now, these barracks had concrete floors, and in his room, there was a bit of a depression near the bed.

"After collecting and storing urine for three weeks, I went to his room one night when he was passed out drunk. I poured that stuff all around his bed . . . ten gallons of it. It was pretty cold in the Carolina's that winter, and the floor was frigid.

"The next morning at reveille, he hit the floor, his feet landed in that cold, stale, stinking piss, and he slipped and fell right on his ass in it. I never even cracked a smile. His room stunk for weeks after that. Funny thing is we're the best of buddies now."

Charles Platt is a very clever fellow whose name will live in the annals of science much like that of Thomas Crapper, the inventor of the toilet. Charles Platt is the father of the Long-range Urine Release Device (LURD). Less cosmopolitan souls than Charles and I would call it a "piss box." But really. . . .

Charles designed his LURD to meet the following needs:

1. A nonviolent, nonhazardous way to saturate the victim with stale urine, in such a way that . . .
2. No personal involvement or appearance of the "gift giver" is required; and . . .
3. The device can be safely sent by mail, turned upside-down, et cetera, without risk of premature urine release.

Here's how it works. First, cut out of stiff cardboard the shapes shown in the illustration. Fold up the sides of the base. Glue the lid together (spread glue on the shaded tab areas). Mount the four razor guards (explanation below) on the base in the positions shown. Get a strong plastic bag (preferably a garbage bag cut down to size) and fill with urine. If available, feel free to add some vomit. Tie the neck of the bag *securely*!

You will now need an old coat hanger, some strong pliers, epoxy glue, and four single-edge razor blades. The blades should be the kind with a metal cap bent over one edge, so they can safely be held. Snip off a few lengths of the coat hanger and use them to brace the razor blades in the corner of the box lid in the positions shown—sharp edges facing down into the lid. The idea is that the blades will slit the bag of urine when the box is opened. Push the bits of coat hanger through the cardboard sides of the lid, cut them off flush, and glue them (apply the glue from the inside only).

Next put the bag of urine into the lid. During this sensitive operation, you must protect the bag from contact with the blades. Do this by slipping little pieces of strong paper in-between. Leave enough of the pieces of paper sticking out so that you can subsequently extract them.

Now slide the sides of the base down into the lid, so they slide between the bag of urine and the sides of the lid. Make sure the

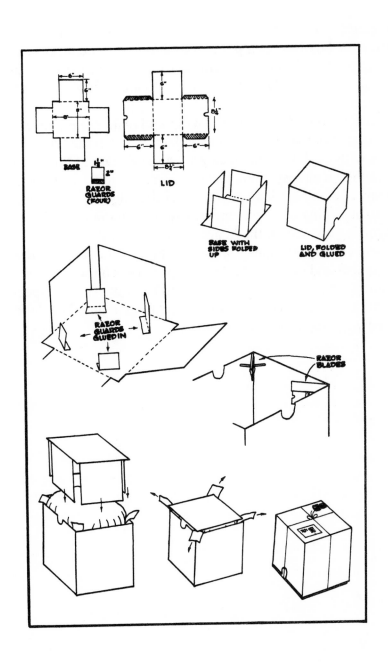

razor guards end up between the urine bag and the blades.

When the box has been put together, pull out the pieces of strong paper which provided temporary protection between the blades and the bag. *This arms the lurd.* It cannot now safely be disassembled.

All you need to do now is gift-wrap and mail. Note that the slicing action of the blades is most effective when the box is opened with the lid section facing up and the base at the bottom. To give the victim psychological encouragement to open the box this way, two half-circles are cut out of the edges of the lid (as shown), providing a convenient way for the victim to hold the box as it is being opened, in the "correct" position.

As soon as the lid slides up, the blades move up beyond the razor guards and cut into the bag. Gaps between the sides of the base allow ample room for the urine to run out. This is especially effective if, for instance, your victim is sitting at an office desk covered with important paperwork. . . .

Vending Machines

Maybe your vending machine served you a rotten meal or took your money and didn't deliver anything. The design of the machine will help you get even. On most machines, when you remove the product, the door stays open. That means you can put something of your own choosing into the machine. Some additions that come readily to mind are: a recapped bottle of pop containing a dead mouse, an old condom, a nicely wrapped sandwich containing dead mice, used Kleenex, sado-porn photos, or Kotex.

Some good street people wrote in to say that No. 14 brass washers are still available in many old-fashioned hardware stores. Cover one side with Scotch tape, trim evenly, and you have an instant dime that cost you a helluva lot less than ten cents.

If you have some reason to rip off a newspaper, you can get free copies of the paper from the older style vending machines. Simply pull hard on the handle and either strike the top of the machine or kick the bottom. It should open for you. If someone sees you, tell them the machine ate your money and didn't deliver as promised. The person will understand.

Or stick "OUT OF ORDER" stickers over the face of every newspaper vending machine you can find. This works well with any vending machine, actually.

Here's a good question from S 'n' M of Ansonia, Connecticut. He wants to know why any trickster would spend good money on brass washers to rip off a newspaper vending machine. He has an easier way.

"Usually, there is a small hole on the tops of these machines. Stick a pin or something thin, strong, and sharp in there, push down, and pull on the door. It will open, and you'll have your paper."

Readers should note that some companies weld over or plug these holes for precisely this reason. But, there are other methods, like No. 14 brass washers.

Venereal Diseases

This basic idea came from several readers and is meant to be an "up yours" style response to any ex-sweetheart or sex date who has given you some physical, social, or mental disease. Here is this nice payback in its generic form.

You call the mark and use the name of Dr. So-and-So of the Department of Health. The mark is informed that his/her name appeared on a list given to the health department by area physicians who have treated these people for venereal disease. You may name a specific strain if you wish. Mexican herpes is a good one.

Usually, the mark is too stunned to do more than stammer denials, but you brush these aside and start asking specific, embarrassing, and personal questions about "who, when, and what." Then you advise the mark to notify all of his or her partners and see a physician as soon as possible for tests.

Keep the telephone number of the real health department handy in case the mark asks about it for verification. Can you imagine someone in that bureaucracy trying to verify a call from a hysterical mark? Great!

This stunt is good to pull on the mark at work, so you can tell the telephone operator, secretary, or receptionist all sorts of good information about this call being of a personal and confidential nature. People have foul minds when it comes to calls from a health department. That's double your fun for one call.

Video Tapes

Herman Kansas wanted to get back at a true sicko-type bully. The bad guy owned a video tape deck, so during a party, Herman placed a couple of small pullet eggs in the cassette slot and slammed it shut. The next day, a video repair guy checked out this mess and eventually charged Senor Bully $250 for the repair work.

As for upsetting TV cameras, Howard Packer says to fire several large flashbulbs directly into the lenses at close range while the video cameras are on. A large strobe unit will work well here. Howard says this wrecks the Vidicon tubes . . . at a very high replacement cost.

Jimi the Z says if any cut-rate video dealer gives you grief beyond reason, simply do your duty as a good citizen and report the store and manager to the FBI for illegally duplicating commercial tapes. Since the Reaganistas halted the FBI from busting corporate and other important crime, the feds now concentrate on rousting video pirates and high school dope smokers.

Visually Handicapped

This is a variation of that old film routine with W.C. Fields as a shopkeeper waiting on a blind man. You can use it to bamboozle those elected old pharts and their toadies who run your municipality as their own fiefdom. You and a friend enter their offices dressed in curious color and design variations, wearing dark glasses, carrying large white canes, and then you start bumping into things. Make demands that the minutes of local board meetings be provided in Braille and that all ordinances be so published.

If your community newspaper is like so many of this country, i.e., a publicity extension of the local merchants, with a Chamber of Commerce mentality, pull the same stunt in their offices. Demand a Braille edition. There is a lot of expensive equipment in newspaper offices, e.g., computer and video display terminals, TV sets, monitors, et cetera. A blind person and his cane can't be held responsible for this damage, especially if the newspaper people are insensitive to their needs. Ho, ho, ho. The only needs many newspaper people are sensitive to are those of the big advertisers.

Zippers

Joe LaTorre suggests a bit of whimsical harassment that could have some real teeth in it. If you have to put up with someone who is appropriately annoying and who also wears a coat with a zipper, he offers an idea.

"Use a pair of pliers to firmly bend the right hand receiver (on a man's coat—reverse for women) just enough so the guide on the other side will not slip into the receiver. Don't leave plier marks, or bend it so much that it is noticeable; just enough so it won't work," Joe suggests.

He also says to be sure and talk to your mark while he or she is trying to get this zapped zipper to work. It makes things more frustrating, especially if you're putting on subtle pressure or acting semi-impatient. Joe calls it a minor irritant, but he says it causes true frustration. I like it.

Zonked

That's what I am from writing all this stuff, and if you've read straight through this far, you deserve to go get zonked on your favorite vice. This is it, the end for this time. As always, I continue to welcome your letters, scams, and rotten stunt ideas for the next book.

And as Roy and Dale always sang at the end of the show, "Happy trails to you . . . until we meet again . . . Happy trails to you. . . ."

"Put an amen to it. There's no more time for praying. Amen!"
——Ethan Edwards, 1868